My Brother's Keeper

One man's harrowing battle to save his brother from addiction

Jack Nolen
&
Katy Newton Naas

HIS Books
Holy Spirit Inspired Stories

Norris City, Illinois

My Brother's Keeper - One Man's Harrowing Battle to Save His Brother from Addiction.
Copyright © 2018 by Jack Nolen and Katy Newton Naas.

Cover photo by Sahray Lydick - Ever After Photography
Cover and interior design by Marilyn Bryant
Other photos provided by family
Edits by Stephanie Taylor

ISBN# 978-0-9989375-6-4

DEDICATION

To Jeff's grandkids, my great nieces and nephews...You've been forced to deal with situations no child should have to. I pray for you every day and hope you use the unfortunate circumstances you've been through as motivation to break the curse of addiction. Each one of you has been made stronger by the hand of adversity you've been dealt and I know God has His hand on you and will bless you if you allow Him to.
– Jack Nolen

To my parents...Thank you for loving us so fiercely, for praying for us, and for believing in us. God knows we didn't always make it easy for you. I will never be able to repay you or thank you enough for your support, through my best days and more importantly, my worst. I love you and I'm so incredibly grateful God chose you for me.
– Katy Newton Naas

A Note from Jack Nolen

Have you ever heard God's still, small voice speak to you about something He wants you to do? If you have and you're like me, the first step in the process is to try to ignore it or pretend it's not actually God's voice. That's how it started for me when God began to deal with me about telling my story by writing a book. Over the years as I've talked with many friends and family members, I've heard countless times the words, "You could write a book with these stories." So when God began telling me that, I just figured it was those conversations and comments resurfacing as I thought about everything that had happened in my life.

In my job, I'm on the road frequently, so I have a lot of alone time while driving. God had me right where He wanted me and He didn't let up. I finally gave in to the fact that writing a book was what God wanted to me to do, so I moved onto the next phase of the project: trying to talk Him out of it. I spent several hours driving several hundred miles down the road, giving Him all the reasons I couldn't put this story into a book. He didn't relent, though, and that still, small voice kept saying, "Yes, you can." One of my arguments for not doing it was I'm not a writer. I don't have the time to write a book and wouldn't have a clue where to start if I did. But if I've learned anything from this process, it's that God sometimes just wants you to give in and when you do, He'll start opening doors and His plan will start falling into place. He doesn't call us to do anything He hasn't already equipped us for. So once I gave in, he began to unfold a plan in front of me. His first answer to my argument that I wasn't a writer was, "No, but you know somebody who is." That somebody was Katy Newton Naas. I've been lifelong friends with Katy's dad and her family and have known her since she was born. Even though her previous books were written for children and teenagers, I knew she was supposed to write this book. I was afraid this would drive her out of her comfort zone and was apprehensive about even approaching her about doing it, so I enlisted the help of the other person besides God who could talk her into it: her dad!

Since this was all part of God's plan, all I really had to do was throw the offer to her and then sit back and let God take care of the rest. He did, of course, and things continued to fall into place. Once Katy got started, she never let up. She endured listening to countless hours of me talking into a voice recorder while driving down the road, and from that, she started to work. Once we sat down and she worked up an outline based off the recording and our more detailed discussions, I don't think there was hardly a day went by that she wasn't working on the book. I know because she would send me text messages or e-mails asking questions or needing more detail on certain things. Thank you, Katy, for everything, and for being who you are!

My hope and prayer is this book touches someone's life and has a positive impact on his or her situation. That maybe somebody will read this and learn from the things I've done and the mistakes I've made and believe me, I've made plenty. Maybe someone will see the same warning signs in someone they're close to and by learning from my mistakes, they'll be able to produce a different outcome. The war against drug addiction is a fight we all have to take up, and nobody has to fight alone. Don't be afraid to speak up and ask for help. Don't keep it to yourself and think it will eventually go away. Trust me, it will probably get worse, much worse. It's too big for any one group to battle alone. It takes law enforcement, the court system, the community, the church, businesses, individuals, and above all else, God. Sometimes by just opening our eyes and being aware of our surroundings, we'll see that there are people all around us who are struggling with an addiction or through someone else's addiction. There aren't many people we come across who haven't been affected by drug addiction in some way. As a matter of fact, I don't personally know anybody. We have to be especially aware of children who may be affected by someone's addiction. They are many times helpless, unable to defend themselves against the perils of addiction and quickly become victims unless someone intervenes on their behalf.

The list of people I need to thank who have impacted my life is too numerous to mention. So many people have had an influence on me along the way, and I am grateful to each and every one. There are a select few who have stuck by me from the start and have overlooked my flaws and shortcomings for a long time – mainly my wife, Lori, my daughter, Tiffany, and my son, Jackson. Dealing with some of the things that have come along hasn't been easy, but you've always been there to help me tackle them. I also want to thank my friend Stan for not only sticking by me all these years, but also for never giving up on my brother. Things would have come off track a long time ago if you hadn't been the counter-balance in his life. Thank you to my stepmother for always being in full support of my dad and taking care of him. As difficult as dealing with Jeff was at times, Dad always had your full support and it made the burden easier than it could have been.

Thank you.

A Note from Katy Newton Naas

When Jack Nolen first approached me about writing this book, I have to admit I hesitated. Not because I didn't want to – Jack is a longtime friend of my dad, and I knew he had a story that needed to be told. But I write books for children and young adults. To take on a project like this, something so completely out of my comfort zone, was daunting. How would I do this story justice? But Jack was so sure I was the right person. "When God began to deal with me about putting this story into a book," he told me, "He intended for you to write it." Who was I to argue with that?

Yet, I still had my doubts. I wanted to write it, but I was terrified. Are you sure, God? Isn't there another author out there better suited for this? I don't know anything about writing a memoir. But I felt a tug, that gentle urging in my heart every time I tried to talk God out of it. I knew God was telling me to help Jack tell his story, and so I agreed. Okay, God, I'll give it a shot. But I'll probably mess it up.

I was right about one thing – I would have messed it up. But once I got out of the way and let God work, things began to fall into place. Shortly after agreeing to the project, I attended a writing conference in Nashville, Tennessee. When I arrived at the conference and picked up the agenda, my jaw dropped. The first session available to me was titled, "The Art and Craft of Memoir." The instructor – an author who wrote memoirs for other people – offered her knowledge of the genre and gave resource after resource while I wrote frantically, recording her every word. The session ended, and I couldn't help but smile. All I had to do was say yes to God, and already He was providing me with what I needed to complete the task. For the next few months, I studied the craft in detail and immersed myself in every memoir I could get my hands on.

I want to thank my co-author, Jack Nolen, for allowing me to be a part of this project. Thank you for believing in me, for trusting me with your story. This book is the result of hours upon hours of interviews, e-mails, phone calls, and text messages – all of which were, I'm confident, emotionally draining and incredibly difficult to relive. Jack's story made me cry and laugh and everything in between, and I am so thankful to be even a small part of it. I also want to thank my family for always being supportive and understanding.

Jack said from the beginning he wanted to share this part of his life in hopes God can use his experiences to help others. His story is proof no one is immune from addiction. Like Jack, I know the powerless, devastating feeling of watching someone you love lose himself to drugs. I have thrown up those desperate prayers and felt like no one heard me. But I'm humbled and overwhelmingly grateful to say I also got to see firsthand what Jesus can do in the life of an addict. When things seem absolutely hopeless, He alone is hope.

Addiction impacts all of us, even if indirectly. It's something no one wants to talk about, but we need to start talking. Drugs not only destroy the lives of those who use them, but their families and friends as well. Too many kids in our schools are suffering in silence at the hands of parents who abuse drugs. Too many mothers, fathers, brothers, and sisters are crying themselves to sleep every night, fearful that when they wake up, the addict they love so desperately won't be with them any longer. I pray this story will encourage those who are living in the dark, suffocating shadows of addiction.

You are not alone.

Table of Contents

Prologue
A Willing Walk into Danger

I eased the truck around the corner and slowed to a stop outside the dilapidated apartment building. The sun's early rays shoved out from behind the hills, warning the darkness that its time was almost up. I took a deep breath and wiped my damp palms on my jeans. It's time. I leaned over and opened the glove box with my eyes still on the apartments, searching for any sign of life upstairs, then wrapped my fingers around the cool steel of my 9mm. I shivered when I glanced down at it and pleaded silently in my head, Lord, please don't make me have to use this. *As comfortable as I felt holding a gun in the woods, tucking one into the waist of my jeans as I prepared to confront a drug dealer somehow didn't bring that same peaceful feeling.*

"Looks like his night visitors have all gone home," my buddy Stan observed from the passenger seat.

I nodded. "Guess that means it's time to make our move." I tried to flash him a grin but didn't quite pull it off.

When I grabbed the door handle, Stan's hand clutched my forearm. "Jack, we don't have to do this."

I sucked in a breath and held it for a moment as I eyed the building again. My brother's face flashed in my mind. I let out the breath in one big whoosh. *"Yeah, we do."*

Stan sighed. "What if it's not in there? What if it's all gone already?"

"It's not." I shook my head. "It's in there. I just know it."

We slipped out of the truck, pushing the doors closed behind us as quietly as we could manage. Stan walked around the truck to join me, and we stared up at the apartment again. I'd never been in the building before, but I knew the layout from my research. Our destination was 2D, in the upper right-hand corner. Stan and I had watched the steady flow of people moving in and out through the darkest hours the night before.

I swallowed. I knew how fast things could go south in a place like this — I'd seen it time and time again as a kid. My heart leapt into my throat.

1

My Brother's Keeper

What were we thinking coming here? Stan was right; we had no way of knowing if we'd even find what we were searching for.

But something in my heart told me we would. We had to. I pulled myself to my full height and squared my shoulders. Though it was my little brother who had gotten us to this point, it felt like my responsibility to fix it. I had to make this right.

I ran my fingers over the gun tucked under my shirt. It was illegal, but I wouldn't dare face this man without it. What...or who...would we find in there? How would he react when we pounded on the door and demanded to be let inside? It was too risky to attempt unarmed.

Stan seemed to read my thoughts. "You sure about this?"

I gave him what I hoped was a confident look. "Let's get this over with." I nodded my head toward the sky. "The sun is about all the way up now. We can't be caught out here in broad daylight."

He took a deep breath. "Okay, then. Let's go."

We moved silently toward the apartment building, our broad steps in unison. We took the old concrete steps two at a time until we reached the balcony of the second floor. My heart raced, but it wasn't from the exertion.

We slid down the hall until we reached the right corner. I stared at the dingy red door. Someone had painted the apartment number near the top; it was chipping off from years of wear, but we could still make out the crooked 2D. I raised my fist and held it there for a moment. God, please be with us. Protect us from what waits on the other side of this door.

Then I knocked.

Chapter One
A Big Brother is Born

I don't remember life before my little brother came along. Mom, Dad, and I spent my earliest years moving around as Dad worked for the Illinois State Police. He started in the northern portion of the state, like most officers do, and worked his way back south to where he grew up. We were just north of Champaign on August 1, 1963, when Jeff was born. At just three years old, I had found my best friend.

I can't recall much from those earliest towns. What I *can* remember is the way I felt when Jeff joined our family. As soon as he was old enough to crawl around after me, we were inseparable.

Dad continued to work his way south, eventually getting all the way to Cairo for a stint before he transferred to Norris City, where I went to kindergarten. We didn't settle permanently until second grade, when we moved to the Ledford community, just south of Harrisburg.

No matter how many times we moved and our surroundings changed, my role as big brother stayed the same. I would be his keeper.

I took that role seriously. When our parents caught us in some typical-boy mischief, I took the punishment for us both without a fight. It was my job to protect Jeff, even when he was old enough to make his own mistakes.

When he was seven, he went to play with one of the neighbor kids. When he didn't come home at five o'clock like he'd promised, Mom and I walked next door. A woman bent over in her garden, yanking weeds from the ground.

"Hello, Glenda. Are Jeff and David here?"

Glenda stood and used the back of her dirty hand to wipe her forehead. "Jeff and David? I thought they were at your house?"

3

Mom frowned. "No, he said they were coming here. You haven't seen him?"

"No, I haven't." She shifted. "David's been gone all afternoon."

Both women went into full-panic mode when they discovered the boys' bikes were gone. When Dad pulled in the driveway around that time, Mom sprinted home.

"Jeff's gone. He took off on his bike without telling me. He said he'd be home at five, but no one's seen him all afternoon."

Dad kept his usual cool composure as he got back into the car. "I'll go hunt him down. I'm sure he's fine. Just lost track of time is all." But I saw the worried creases in his forehead when he threw the car in reverse.

Even Dad was nervous? My heart leapt into my throat. Dad was the strongest, bravest man I knew. If he was scared, I knew I should be, too. I wanted to run after him, to stop him and demand he take me with him. But I knew he'd tell me to stay home with Mom, to keep her calm.

So, I plopped down in the front yard. It seemed like hours before Dad's car came back into view, and I leapt to my feet. A relieved sigh escaped when I saw Jeff's head poke up from the back seat.

When Dad parked, he got out of the car without looking at me and pulled the back door open. "Inside. Now."

Jeff inched his way out of the car, his body tense and alert. He ducked his head, his shoulders curled forward, and dragged his feet to the house.

Uh oh. I recognized that look in Dad's eyes. I'd seen it myself a few times, and I knew what usually accompanied it. *Jeff's getting a spanking.*

Tears burned behind my eyes. What did he do? Where did he go? What could have been so important that he lied about where he was and ignored his curfew?

I hurried through the front door, searching for any excuse I could make on his behalf. Jeff's pleas for mercy echoed from the kitchen. I couldn't stand the thought of Dad whipping Jeff, even if he deserved it. But though I racked my brain as I ran toward them, I couldn't think of anything to stop it.

"Wait!" I burst into the room. "Don't spank him."

4

Dad's head jerked toward me. His eyes narrowed.

I swallowed. "He's just a little kid. Spank me instead."

Dad sighed and shook his head. "Stay out of this, Jack. It doesn't concern you."

"Yes, it does. I…I told him to go off on his bike. It's…my fault."

Jeff's head jerked up in surprise. Dad's eyes shifted between Jeff and me. "What do you mean, it's your fault?"

I took a bold step toward them. "I was the one who told him he could go off on his bike. If you're gonna whip somebody, whip me."

Dad's gaze withered me. I trembled under it.

He shook his head. I could see the disappointment in his eyes, something that crushed me so much more than the thought of angering him ever could. If there was one person I didn't want to let down, it was Dad. "Get on out of here before I have to whip you both – him for being out where he's not supposed to be, and you for lying to me."

But I had to help Jeff. My mouth opened, though I didn't know what else to say. When Dad's hand came up to whip Jeff, I leapt between them, throwing myself over Jeff's body like a momma bear protecting her cub just before his big hand came down.

I took that spanking. It stung, but I didn't regret it. I held my head high, knowing I did my job – I protected my brother.

And then Dad calmly picked me up, moved me aside, and spanked Jeff anyway.

As we grew together, our bond did, too – though we couldn't always find a lot in common, and sometimes we didn't understand each other.

My life as a kid revolved around sports seasons – basketball in the winter, baseball in the summer, and football in the fall. I lived for them all. Baseball held a special place in my heart as Dad coached our team. I put my heart and soul into becoming the best player I could be. I loved it, but what I loved most about it was the time I got to spend with my dad. All I wanted was to make him proud.

Jeff, on the other hand, had very little interest in sports. His greatest love was horses. Mom and Dad got him one, and he rode it every day. He played a little basketball in grade school, but only to be with his friends. As for baseball, he just didn't care about it the way I did. He actually had a lot of athletic ability and even tried out for the baseball team one summer and made it, only to quit the very next day.

I was shocked. All that work? We were supposed to spend the summer together playing baseball. And the look on Dad's face when he told him he quit...how could he? When I asked him why, he shrugged. "I don't know. It's just not my thing."

I stared at him. "Then why did you try out in the first place?"

When he shrugged again, his casual smirk on his face, I decided not to push it any further. But in my mind, I wondered about it often. Did he feel pressured into trying out? Did he just want to prove he could make the team?

Despite our differences, we had one common love: the outdoors. We spent every long summer day outside together, usually toting BB guns. Mom's parents lived just down the road, and Grandpa took us fishing and hunting. We loved those days we spent with him, just the three of us in the wild.

Grandpa passed away when I was thirteen years old, and his absence left a void in our lives. We missed our time with him, missed our adventures at the pond and especially in the woods. When he died, he took a piece of us with him. We belonged out there in that tree stand. We needed someone else to take us.

Jeff approached Dad first. "Dad, will you take us hunting?" Dad sighed. "Maybe another weekend." He didn't share our passion for nature, and he definitely didn't know much about hunting. His own father died in a mining accident when he was only ten years old, leaving him and his four siblings to be raised by their mother. He didn't grow up running through the country hills like Jeff and I did – he never had the chance to be the kind of kid who ran barefoot through the grass, carrying a fishing pole. He became the man of the house at an early age.

But we didn't give up. As soon as deer season approached, we started begging. Day after day, we pleaded with him, sure we would wear him down. He offered excuses for weeks. And then one Friday, when he looked in our imploring eyes, something softened. "Okay. We'll go tomorrow morning."

Chapter One - A Big Brother Is Born

Our screams must have echoed through the whole neighborhood. We sprinted around the house, high-fiving and jumping on the couch in victory. When we climbed in bed early that night and set our alarm for three a.m., we still couldn't wipe the smiles from our faces.

Neither of us slept. My stomach danced in anticipation as I checked the alarm every hour. We shut it off long before it ever sounded. My heart raced as I pulled on my camo coveralls in the dark bedroom. "You think Dad will get a deer?"

Jeff shrugged. "Nah. He's never even been hunting."

"Doesn't matter. He knows how to shoot. I bet he'll be good at it."

He nodded. "Yeah, you're probably right."

We tried to tiptoe to the kitchen but giggled the whole way there, waking Dad. He wore a smile as he packed peanut butter and jelly sandwiches and chips, and I knew he was as excited for our adventure as we were.

We picked up my uncle and cousin before we headed to the woods. Dad put me in a stand by myself, then took Jeff with him a couple hundred yards away. My chest puffed out against my coveralls. Dad trusted me to be alone out there.

After an entire day in the woods, not one of us got a deer, not even Dad. But Jeff and I didn't care. Just holding the gun in my hands, smelling the pine around me while the cold wind whipped against my face – it was like coming home. Knowing my dad and brother were out there beside me made it perfect.

I realized later Dad didn't care much for it. But he pretended to, for the chance to spend time with us. He began taking us regularly. Some of my best memories from my childhood are from those chilly days in the woods. Jeff and I looked forward to deer season every year, talking about it months before it arrived, driving Mom and Dad insane with our constant countdowns and planning.

Squirrel season was also highly anticipated in our house – it started on August 1, Jeff's birthday. We would pack up and head out into the woods, where we spent a couple days camping and hunting in the hot summer sun before we had to go back to school. As we got older, we were allowed to camp out by ourselves. We felt like real men, being out in the woods, just the two of us. I can't recall the details of those late-night conversations around campfires, but I can still remember the way it made me feel. Being out there, Jeff and I didn't have a care in the world. We were happy. Safe. We were more than brothers; we were best friends. As long as we had each other, we had it all.

I had no idea at the time how easy it would be to lose it.

Chapter Two
A House Divided

Dad went into the Department of Criminal Investigation when I was ten years old. In his new role as detective, he covered the southern sixteen counties of Illinois. It seemed there was always a burglary or homicide that called him away on the weekends. My fascination with his career only solidified his hero status in my eyes. I was amazed by his stories and wanted to be right in the middle of it all. Dad took me with him many weekends, letting me sit in the car or dropping me at the local police department or sheriff's office while he worked. I was ten feet tall riding in the car next to him.

Those weekends left a lasting impression on me. I got to see firsthand what drugs and alcohol could do. Weekend after weekend, I saw families torn apart by addiction-fueled crime. I also got to see my dad in action. I watched him question suspects through a two-way mirror in the local sheriff's office. I hung on to his every word. What struck me every time was the way he treated those people, always with respect. I believe that was one of the main reasons he was so successful at his job – it was like they couldn't help but confide in him, couldn't help but confess their crimes.

Though Dad thrived in his role as detective, just three years after he started that position, Grandpa's death brought changes to our home. Mom sank into a bit of a depression. She tried to carry on as usual, but she couldn't get past her father's death, and it affected everything she did. Jeff, who wasn't interested in Dad's job and chose not to go with us on the weekends, stayed home with her. I could see her sadness wearing off on Jeff and could see his own attitude changing with each passing day.

Between Dad's traveling and Mom's struggles, they began to

grow apart. Even when Dad was home, the distance between them seemed to grow wider. There was less laughter in our house. And more arguments. A divide began to settle in our house, pulling Jeff and I right along with it, though we didn't realize it at the time.

Mom always took us to church and Sunday school. She tried her best to teach us good morals, and no matter what was going on between her and Dad, the one thing they agreed on was instilling in us the value of hard work. It had been passed down to them by their own parents. I remember Grandpa telling us when we were young if we wanted money in our pockets, we better be ready to work for it. Mom and Dad adopted that same attitude, and it rubbed off on me. I got my first job at twelve years old, working at the town pool. I rode my bike to get there every day. I spent many summers working on farms, detasseling corn in the field or hauling hay. I took pride in my work, took pride in knowing anything extra I had was from putting my time and energy into giving a job everything I could.

Jeff didn't spend his summers working. He just didn't require much and didn't seem to feel that pull to have a job. He was content to run around the neighborhood with the other Ledford boys. Some of them didn't have the best reputation. I didn't worry much about Jeff as long as his good friend, Stan, was around. Stan and Jeff were the same age and had been in the same class since kindergarten. Like Jeff, he got into a little mischief now and then, but he had a good head on his shoulders. I knew if Jeff tried to get into anything too crazy or dangerous, Stan would keep him in check. And in our small town, it was hard to do anything without the whole population talking about it. Jeff was smart enough not to fall in too deep with the wrong crowd.

I wasn't blind to the tension at home, but I guess between work, sports, and hunting, I was too busy to see just how big the gap between Mom and Dad had become. Or maybe I just chose not to see it.

But when Dad sat Jeff and me down just three days before my sixteenth birthday to tell us he was moving out, I couldn't ignore it anymore. My mouth opened, then closed, then opened again. I had no words. *No, you can't leave,* I wanted to tell him. *This is just a rough patch, that's all. You'll get through it. You have to.* But when I saw his suitcase by the door, I kept my pleas to myself. This wasn't a rash decision made after an argument; it had been coming for years.

When I watched him pull out of the driveway, something squeezed inside my chest. Jeff and I stood next to each other, neither of us saying a word, as he drove away. Mom shut herself in the bedroom and an eerie silence settled in the house that night. That squeezing in my chest moved into my throat, relentless, until I felt suffocated. I climbed into my bed that night, not even bothering to pull down the covers, and stared at the ceiling until the morning light peeked in through the curtains.

✵ ✵ ✵ ✵

Though my world stopped for a bit, time didn't stop with it.

Dad settled in a house across town. His salary wasn't enough to sustain two households, so for the first time in her life, Mom went to work. She first got a job at the gift shop in the local hospital before becoming an insurance clerk at Peabody Coal. Dad continued to travel frequently as an Illinois State Police detective.

Jeff and I learned to split our time between Mom and Dad, though the animosity between them made it difficult. Mom's bitterness toward Dad spilled over into everything she did, including parenting Jeff and me. She couldn't talk about Dad without badmouthing him, and it affected us and our relationship with our father. I found myself angry with him and avoiding him for weeks at a time.

Dad knew what was happening. One particular visit, when Jeff and I were icy toward him, he sat down on the couch and put his head in his hands for a moment before he sighed and stood up, his eyes darting back and forth between both of us. "Boys, I know you're upset with me. But I need you to understand one thing: there are two sides to every story. Your mom, she has her side of it and for whatever reason, she feels the need to share her pain with you two. I'm not going to do that. But I hope you will think about it, *really* think about it, and understand that this situation…it's not as simple as it may seem. There's more to it, you know?"

My Brother's Keeper

His words penetrated my heart. I thought about what he said the rest of the night and decided right then and there I wasn't going to let my mom's anger with him poison me any longer. This was my *dad*, after all, my hero. He wasn't perfect, and neither was Mom, but I knew how much they both loved us, despite their mistakes. From that moment on, I wouldn't choose sides. I would love them both through their flaws.

For whatever reason, Dad's words didn't impact Jeff the way they did me. He continued to treat Dad with contempt. It seemed easy for him to side with Mom – he never really bonded with Dad the way I did, despite our hunting excursions. His anger with Dad only seemed to fuel his desire to buck authority however he could.

Life as we once knew it was over, and we eventually settled into our new life with relative ease, all things considered. But with this new life came freedom – too much freedom. Especially in the summer months when school no longer consumed our days.

Summer nights turned chilly, and on September 6, 1976, I turned sixteen. Dad had bought a 1965 Willys Jeep the year before to use for hunting and riding in the woods. The brakes weren't very reliable – in fact, more often than not, they didn't work at all – but when I got my license, it became mine anyway. It didn't go over fifty miles per hour, and I actually became really good at driving without brakes; I learned to start down-shifting long before I got to a stop sign. I often took Jeff with me when I went anywhere. I can't count how many times we would be riding along and suddenly need brakes that basically didn't exist and drove out into fields, jumped ditches, swerved into yards or rolled through stop signs. Luckily, no one ever got hurt and nothing got torn up, so we always got a good laugh out of it. We'd get them fixed, and they'd last a few days before they went out again.

When Jeff wasn't with me, he ran with his friends, becoming more and more rebellious. He started skipping school and his grades declined so that at the end of his eighth grade year, he found himself unable to move on to high school. The news crushed me – I looked forward to him being a freshman while

I was a senior. We would finally be in high school together. But Jeff seemed unfazed. He didn't care about school, didn't see the importance of writing papers or solving math equations or even progressing from one grade level to the next.

Skipping school left his days free to find more mischief to get into. At only thirteen, he couldn't drive, so he rode a lawnmower around town until he wore out the engine. In an area like Ledford, there weren't a lot of things to do, so Jeff and his friends passed their time by playing pranks throughout the neighborhood. When a certain group of men spent evenings sitting around a campfire, drinking, Jeff and his buddies hid in the nearby woods and shot bottle rockets toward them. Another night, they put a coffee can over a smoking chimney so the smoke went back into the house, terrifying the residents. One morning, they put a stray cat in a random mailbox about two hours before the mail deliveries were made. They hid in some nearby bushes and watched for the unsuspecting mailman to pull up to the mailbox and yank open the door, laughing hysterically when the cat sprinted out and ran straight up his arm. He got in the mailman's car, scratching and clawing at him with wild rage after being cooped up in the small space for so long. Stunts like those made Jeff and his friends almost notorious around town.

When he did decide to attend school, he couldn't show up without causing some sort of ruckus. Most of the time, he got started before he even got there – stirring up trouble on school bus number fifty. He wasn't alone in this; it had to be at least once a week that during first hour over the intercom system, the secretary would end the daily announcements by saying, "All students who ride bus number fifty, please come to the office." Someone on the bus was always being scolded for some sort of misbehavior. One particular day, Jeff decided to play with a lighter in the back of the bus and managed to catch the seat on fire. He was trying to burn off the strings where part of the seat had unraveled, and the whole thing went up like a brush pile. Fortunately, the bottom cushion part of the seat popped loose, so the driver was able to unclip it and throw it out the emergency exit before anyone got hurt. "Who did this?" The bus driver scanned the faces in the back row. "Somebody better start talking." But no one would rat Jeff out. All four boys in the back row refused to tell on him, even when the principal demanded it, and each one of them took four swats with a paddle before first hour even began.

I knew Jeff was taking a dark turn, but I didn't intervene much. I told myself it was temporary, that his rebellion was normal given the fact that our family had been ripped apart. *He'll get it together,* I told myself. *We all do stupid things. We're kids — that's what we're supposed to do, right?* I didn't let myself worry about him. His pranks seemed harmless enough. No one had been hurt. He was just having some fun.

I almost looked forward to hearing what crazy story he would come home with each evening. And for a little while, I even let myself get sucked into their schemes…until one brush with the law became a little too much.

Chapter Three
Corn Kernels and Oil

The Ledford community is a four-mile stretch of land along Route Forty-Five, settled between Harrisburg and Carrier Mills. The sparsely-populated land is covered in hills and mounds from old strip mining operations. Growing up here had its perks – one of which being the freedom that comes with living in a relatively safe area. That freedom allowed our group of local boys to run around together, day or night, without a whole lot of supervision. Downfalls accompanied that, too; when we found some harmless mischief or caused a little ruckus, most people knew exactly who the culprits were.

Halloween season was our favorite time to have a little fun with our Ledford neighbors. We spent hours sitting around with corn cobs, pulling off individual kernels of corn and tossing them into buckets. As I was the only one with a license, I was nominated to haul the other boys around to throw the kernels at houses and cars. Our favorite nighttime activity was to get on top of the old railroad tresses where the road ran through and throw corn at the cars that passed under. We actually made it a mission to get the police called on us – there were a couple houses nearby with residents who were sure to do so when we threw a little corn at their siding. We'd get on the tresses and watch for the police car to approach. When it did, someone would shout, "Ready... now!" Then we pelted the car with corn. The cop, of course, was sure to come to an abrupt halt. He would get out and scream at us while we sprinted at full speed and hid in the woods.

One particular Friday night that year, a local deputy decided he wasn't going to tolerate our pranks any longer. When he showed up at the railroad tresses and got out of the car, he didn't cross his arms over his chest and give us the verbal what-for like he usually did. Instead, he chased us toward the woods, screaming the whole way. "That's it! If I get called out here after you boys just *one more time,* I'll make examples out of all of you! I'll take you straight to jail! Do you hear me?"

His strides were no match for a bunch of young boys. We giggled the whole way into the woods, delighting in his threats, and threw ourselves behind the nearest brush piles. He gave up before he even got into the woods, but before he left, he shouted one last time. "I mean it. One more time! Just try me!"

To a group of thirteen- to sixteen-year-old boys, his words were an invitation to step up our game.

The next morning, Stan strolled in the house bright and early. He came straight to the room Jeff and I shared, waking us both. "Get up. We've got a plan."

Jeff and I threw on some clothes and followed him out of the house. Jeff practically skipped beside me. "So what're we gonna do?"

Stan grinned. "Jack, you gotta take us down to where that old mining equipment is. You remember that oil?"

My eyes narrowed. Of course I remembered the fifty-five gallon barrel of gear oil that sat out there. "What about it?"

"We're gonna haul it to the tresses."

I laughed. "Who is?"

"We are." Stan waggled his eyebrows. "Just gotta run by and get Thomas and Brandon."

We piled in my Jeep and went down the road to pick up our buddies. On the way there, Stan informed us of the plan: we would throw old tires up the path between the road and the tresses, then let the oil drain down the hill to soak them and everything on the trail. We'd park the Jeep about three-quarters of a mile from the tresses, where we would be throwing corn. When the cop got out to chase us up that path, he'd be sure to fall and get covered in oil.

"That's genius," Jeff said, giving Stan a congratulatory slap on the back.

"It is pretty brilliant, actually," I had to admit. "Let's do it."

Thomas was already waiting in his front yard when we pulled up. He jumped in, and we moved on around the circle to let

Brandon get in, too, then headed straight to the old mining equipment.

Minutes later, the five of us stood around the giant barrel. We had to park several hundred feet away, as the land was too rough for my old Jeep to navigate. "Let's just roll it over there and strap it in," Thomas suggested. "It's too heavy to carry it over all these rocks."

That's exactly what we did. We all took our positions around the barrel and eased it over the rocks and hills until we reached the Jeep. Then we lifted it up into the back, strapped it in, and collapsed to the ground for a bit. After a few moments to recover, we tossed a few old tires in after it and then jumped in the Jeep to head over to the railroad tresses.

We unloaded the barrel at the bottom of the hill. It seemed bigger than it had been the day before. We stared up at it, then looked down at the heavy barrel at our feet. Brandon shook his head. "This ain't gonna be easy."

"Just think about the look on the cop's face when he falls face-first in that oil." Jeff grinned. "That'll make it a little easier."

We all laughed, then worked together to shove the barrel onto its side. We stood shoulder-to-shoulder and braced ourselves to fight it up the hill. And inch by inch, we moved it to the top of the hill, grunting and sweating the whole way up. When we finally reached our destination, we cheered. Jeff and I hurried back down to the bottom, grabbed the tires, and scattered them along the path on our way to the top.

"You know, I...I think I've got another idea," Stan said when we reached the top. His eyebrows furrowed in concentration. "We could step this thing up."

"What do you have in mind?" I asked.

"Well, no matter who the cop is, they always seem to do the same thing: stop right down there, throw the car in park and just get out and start running after us without even shutting the car off."

We nodded.

Stan grinned. "What if one of us was hiding in the ditch down there? Then as soon as the cop started up the hill and hit that oil, he could run out, jump in the police car, and take off with it?"

Jeff, Brandon, and Thomas immediately laughed and started high-fiving each other. I smiled with them, but inside, my stomach turned. Stealing a police car? I didn't know about that. Throwing a little corn was one thing. Dumping the oil to trip the cop up a little bit…even that was a little out of my comfort zone, but it was harmless enough. But stealing his car? My dad's face popped into my mind. What would he think about this? Despite our Halloween pranks, I actually had great respect for law enforcement. I knew how hard my dad worked, knew how he dedicated his whole life to protecting and serving. I admired the men who gave themselves to the job like he did.

Stan seemed to read my thoughts. He clasped my shoulder. "Hey, I'm not suggesting we take it out joy riding or anything. Let's just take it down to the cemetery. Whoever's driving it could leave it there and jump it with us."

I nodded. The cemetery was just a quarter mile away from the tresses. "Well…okay. I guess that wouldn't hurt anything."

When we were satisfied with our plan and had everything in place, we left. We came back that evening and hid the Jeep behind a large hill, then walked the half mile to the tresses with a bucket of corn kernels in tow.

"If getting the cops called is our goal, we might as well start over there," Jeff said, nodding toward the nearest house. The lady who lived there was known to call them as soon as we started our hijinks.

We all nodded in agreement and made our way toward her house, whooping and hollering as we went. The first handful of corn kernels flew from one of the boys behind me, sprinkling her siding like rain. Before the next one could follow, we heard her voice from inside the house. "You boys better get on out of here – I'm calling the cops!"

We cheered and threw a few more handfuls of corn just to make sure she would go through with it, then ran back to the tresses. Thomas jumped in the ditch at the bottom of the path while the rest of us stood on top with more corn in hand. It wasn't long before we spotted the red and blue flashing lights in the distance. My heart beat so wildly I thought it would pound right out of my chest.

Chapter Three - Corn Kernels and Oil

As luck would have it, the same deputy from the night before was driving the car. He screeched to a halt and jumped out of the car — leaving it running, the driver's side door wide open, with the lights still flashing. My stomach leapt into my throat. This was normally the time we would sprint toward the woods to hide. But that night, we held our ground. Instead of running away, we tossed our corn kernels down toward him.

"Come get us!" we taunted.

What happened next was like a scene from a movie. The deputy ran for the path, just as we had hoped. As soon as he hit the oil, he slid and fell, soaking his uniform up the back. While he cursed and tried to get to his feet, Thomas popped out of the ditch. He dove into the open driver's seat and threw it in drive while we cheered above him. "Go, go, go!"

I took my eyes off Thomas when I noticed the deputy back on his feet, carefully moving toward us once again. "You guys, let's go!" I elbowed Jeff and pointed at the oil-smeared face staring up at us.

We sprinted to the Jeep. When everyone was in, I floored it until we reached the cemetery. I parked, shut off the engine, and scanned the area. "Where's Thomas?"

I could feel each second tick by while we all searched for him. "He said he'd meet us here, right?" Stan asked.

"If he doesn't get here soon, we gotta leave," Brandon said. "We can't let that cop see your Jeep."

Jeff shook his head. "We aren't leaving without him. He'll show up. Just stay here."

We continued to comb the area with our eyes. I just knew that deputy was going to appear in front of us, ready to walk us all to jail. How would I explain this to Dad?

When I saw a figure running toward us, I swallowed hard. *This is it. We're busted.* But as he got closer, I squinted, then sighed in relief. "There he is! There's Thomas!"

I turned the key and the engine roared to life just as Brandon opened the back door and Thomas dove inside. We drove until we reached our hiding spot nearby, behind a group of trees and mounds. I shut off the engine and killed the lights. None of us breathed a word. The only sound I could hear was Thomas's panting until Stan finally mumbled, "Thomas, where's the cop car?"

He sucked in a breath. "At the Baptist Church."

We all turned to look at him. The Baptist Church was only about a hundred yards from where he stole it in the first place. I frowned. "The Baptist Church? Why'd you go there?"

He shook his head. "I don't know. It was like, it just hit me, you know? All you guys did was throw a little corn. But I stole a police car! If anyone was gonna get in trouble, it was me, right?" He sighed and shook his head again. "I just had to get out of there."

Stan's eyes were wide. "So you ran all the way here? That's, like, over a mile away."

"Yep."

We all stared at him in disbelief until a grin spread over Jeff's face. When he giggled, we all burst into quiet laughter, Thomas included, until the whole Jeep shook along with us. My cheeks ached as several minutes went by and none of us could contain our almost-silent cackles.

The headlights that flashed nearby were enough to wipe the smiles off all our faces. We froze, moving nothing but our eyes as we watched those lights comb the woods and the hills all around us. For over an hour, we stayed like that, too scared to do anything but breathe.

Finally, Jeff dared to whisper. "You guys, I haven't seen anything for a while. I think it's safe to get out of here."

I wasn't so sure, but the other guys agreed. "It'll be fine." Stan reached up from the back seat to give my shoulder a reassuring slap. "Just don't turn your lights on."

The engine seemed louder than ever when I started it up again. I cringed, my eyes darting from one side to the other, sure those headlights were going to reappear and land on us. When they didn't, I inched my way forward, unable to see through the dark and thin patches of fog.

We crawled forward for what seemed like hours before we reached the gravel road, where I finally felt safe enough to turn the lights on again. I let out a breath I hadn't even realized I was holding as we cruised down the familiar route toward home.

Still no one spoke. I tried to lean against the seat, pretending to be casual, but the tension stayed in my shoulders. Was that deputy still out searching? Would he know it was us? If he pulled me over, would our faces betray our secret?

I relaxed a little when we turned down Brandon's road to take him home. We dropped off Thomas next, then Stan. With just Jeff in the Jeep beside me, I finally allowed myself to smile. "I can't believe we pulled that off."

Jeff smirked. "We're not home yet."

When we walked inside, we found Mom perched on the couch. She leapt to her feet as soon as she saw us. "It's getting late, boys. Where've you been?"

Jeff and I exchanged glances. He bit his inner cheek, trying to suppress a smile. A snort of laughter escaped my mouth. Jeff's wide grin spread over his face.

Mom tried to glare at us, but her lips twitched, giving away her amusement. "Okay. Somebody better start talking."

Jeff and I stared at each other for a moment. Jeff gave me a slight nod. I looked at Mom. "Promise you won't get mad?"

She crossed her arms over her chest. "No. But you better tell me anyway."

I nodded. "Fine. You better sit down for this."

Raising her eyebrows, she lowered herself onto the middle of the couch. Jeff and I plopped down on either side of her. For the next ten minutes, she listened while we took turns relaying the whole story, starting with our planning session earlier that day. Her face registered various degrees of shock as we shared each detail. Our voices grew as the tension rose, and we interrupted each other in our excitement, each one eager to boast in our genius and cunning.

When we finished, Mom's hands flew to her cheeks, her fingertips white from pressing against her face. "I...I can't believe..." She dropped her hands into her lap and shook her head. "Now, Jeff, I might have expected something like this from you. But Jack? You really went along with all this?"

I shrugged, feeling a little smaller. "It was just a harmless prank, Mom. No one got hurt."

As soon as the words left my mouth, three short knocks made

us all jump. "Police," a muffled voice said behind the door.

Jeff, Mom, and I scrambled to our feet and stared at each other, our eyes wide. My pulse throbbed in my throat. *Was this it? Were we busted?* I wasn't surprised the cops were out looking for us or even that they stopped at our house – in a town that size, the list of potential suspects was pretty small. But did they know it was us? Did we leave something behind, something to prove our guilt?

Mom squared her shoulders and smoothed her brown hair before she strolled to the door. When she pulled it open, she pasted on a smile. "Hello, officer. It's awfully late for a visit, isn't it? Can I help you with something?"

"Yes, ma'am. We're sorry to bother you at this time of night, but we're looking for Jack and Jeff Nolen."

For a moment, my heart seemed to stop. Jeff and I stared at each other, frozen in the middle of the living room.

"My boys? They're both here. What do you need with them?"

"Have they been home long, ma'am?"

"Have they been home long? Yes, they've been here all night, actually. In fact, we just finished watching a movie. We've got a little popcorn left, if you'd like some."

My jaw dropped. Jeff's eyes lit up and his signature grin reappeared. He motioned toward the couch, and together we crept toward it, each taking a seat on either end.

"All night?" the deep voice in the doorway repeated.

"Yes, sir. I don't get quality time with my sons often. I have to say I've really enjoyed the evening."

Jeff and I just looked at each other in awe. It was the first time I'd ever heard my mother just flat-out *lie* to someone. And to a cop, of all people!

When the officer was satisfied a few moments later, Mom shut the door behind him, then turned back toward Jeff and me. She leaned against the wall, staring at us as if gathering her thoughts, then started toward us, her chin jutting in the air. I took a deep breath to brace myself for what I knew was coming. I'd seen that look in her eye more than once; Jeff and I were in for the scolding of a lifetime.

She stood in front of the couch, her arms folded tightly across her chest. "What you boys did tonight...it was...idiotic. It was disrespectful and downright dangerous. Someone could have been hurt. What if you'd been caught? We'd be having a very different conversation when I came to pick you up from the police station."

I ducked my head. "I know, Mom. It was...stupid. I'm sorry." When I heard her sniffling, my head jerked up. "Oh, Mom, we didn't mean to..."

But when her eyes met mine, I realized she wasn't crying. Her shoulders shook, but her face seemed almost...

"Mom, are you laughing?" Jeff's incredulous voice echoed my own question.

She put her hand over her mouth and composed herself. "It's not funny. It's really not. It's just...when I picture that cop trying to run up the hill, his uniform soaked in that oil, I can't..." And she melted into giggles all over again.

Jeff and I couldn't help but chuckle. She fell onto the couch between us and the three of us laughed until our stomachs ached.

Finally, she forced the smile from her face. "I want you to know that I...just because I'm laughing doesn't mean I approve. You should have known better than to go along with something like that. Especially you, Jack. You're supposed to be the older one, the responsible one, the voice of reason."

The smile fell from my face. "I know, Mom. Don't worry. I won't do anything like that again."

She nodded, her eyes serious, but the corners of her mouth still curled up a little.

Though we got a good laugh out of it, I meant what I said when I told Mom I wouldn't do anything like that again.

But Jeff? He was only getting started.

Chapter Four
Growing Up

Mom and Dad's hostile divorce dragged on over a year. I finished high school, completing my senior year without my little brother in the building with me. Jeff went to eighth grade for the second year, this time showing up enough days to scrape by and pass. It was during that year he started smoking cigarettes and soon after, pot. He started high school the following fall, but told me the first day he was only going to get his driver's license. He still cared nothing about his grades and at the end of the year, he found himself held back again.

Meanwhile, fresh out of high school, I got a job at a food distribution warehouse loading food to deliver to grocery stores in the tristate area. I worked there for about six months before I took a position as a coal miner at Sahara Coal Company in February 1979. Dad wasn't thrilled with my new career – he had lost his own father in a mining accident – but safety underground had improved over the years, and the pay was good. For a kid just out of high school who had no plans of going to college, it was one of the most popular options.

Jeff went back to school to start his freshman year over. He turned sixteen in August and continued going to school only long enough to get his driver's license, then quit the very next day. Mom and Dad didn't approve of his decision but got him an old car to drive anyway.

That's around the time things really began to spiral out of my control.

Though the divorce was finalized, Mom still couldn't find a way to get past her anger toward my dad. She continued to say nasty things about him to Jeff and me, and while I remembered Dad's words and kept in mind that there were two sides to the story, Jeff seemed to buy into every word she said. His resentment toward Dad seemed to spark a hatred toward all policemen and authority, and his pranks went from harmless to serious law-breaking stunts almost overnight. He started shoplifting – first small things, like candy from convenience stores, just to see if he could get away with it. When he realized he could, he got braver in his quests, going into Walmart and lifting larger items, like tools. In the beginning, he showed me his new stolen items with pride. After I scolded him, he stopped bragging about his theft victories to me, though it didn't stop him from stealing. I didn't understand it – he showed no remorse for what he was doing, didn't even seem to realize his actions were wrong.

He started running with a bad crowd, not coming home when he was supposed to and not even telling where or when he was going. Mom couldn't handle him, but she refused to call Dad for help. Instead, she relied on me. On weekend nights, I would ride through town, asking around until I found out where he was, and then Mom and I would go after him. We often found him in bad areas, in houses known for drugs or violence. At that point, I still had enough bluff on him to coax him home, usually by threatening to beat his butt if he didn't come with us. Weekend after weekend, I yanked him out of places he didn't need to be and took him home.

Sometimes when I thought about the turn his life had taken, I just sat down and cried. Who was this angry kid, this pot-smoking thief? Where had my little brother gone? I felt lost. My best friend was slipping through my fingertips, and I had no idea what to do about it.

One evening I came home from work to find him pacing in the living room. One look at the worried crease in his forehead, and my heart sank. "Jeff? What's wrong?"

He stopped in the middle of the floor and sighed. "It's Kimberly."

I didn't really know Kimberly, his girlfriend of a few months. I had seen her a few times, but only when I went to drag Jeff home on Saturday nights. "What about her?"

He ran his hands through his short light-brown hair. "She's pregnant."

Chapter Four - Growing Up

"Wow." I raised my eyebrows. "It's yours?"

Jeff frowned. "Of course it's mine."

I put my hands up in surrender. "Sorry. I didn't know if…" I ambled to the couch and sank into it. "What are you gonna do, bud?"

"Well…" He sighed again. His eyes dropped to the ground, and he shoved his hands in his pockets before he dragged his feet toward the couch to join me. "Marry her, I guess. Is that what I'm supposed to do?"

I shook my head, my eyes wide. "I don't know. I mean, I guess it's probably the right thing to do. But…you're only sixteen, Jeff. You don't…have a job."

"So I'll get one." He shrugged. "Someone said they're looking for some help over at the lumber yard in Carrier Mills. Maybe I'll go there."

I nodded. "That'd be a good start."

Even in the midst of my shock, it crossed my mind that maybe this pregnancy was a blessing in disguise. Just hearing Jeff talk about settling down, getting a job…it gave me hope. Sure, he was young, but maybe this baby would be the push he needed to get his head on straight. *Finally, he's going to grow up. We can stop worrying about him all the time,* I thought. *All this running around with bad crowds is going to stop.*

He went to the lumber yard and got that job he had heard about. A month later, he and Kimberly were married, and they moved into the camper that set in Grandma's yard just down the road. Jeff turned seventeen in August, and their daughter, Christina, was born in December.

The day they brought Christina home, I went to visit them. I held my niece in my arms, in awe of her tiny fingers, her long eyelashes, of how fierce my love for her grew with every passing second. Before I left that evening, I went to the kitchen for a glass of water. When I came out, I found Jeff alone with Christina, holding her in his lap, his hands cradling her delicate head as she stared up at him, her eyes wide. "We're going to have so many adventures," he whispered. "I'll take you fishing and hunting. We'll spend hours in the outdoors, just you and me." He leaned down and kissed her nose. "I will give you the whole

27

world."

I smiled and tiptoed out of the room, unable to bring myself to interrupt that moment to even say goodbye. Peace rested in my chest. *He's going to be just fine.*

Parenthood didn't settle the pair down right away. Anyone could see just by watching Jeff with Christina how much he loved her. But he and Kimberly were so young. They longed for their old days of staying out all night, drinking and smoking pot, living without a care.

I saw it. I knew he hadn't changed completely, but I tried to shrug it off. *He's young. He'll get it out of his system soon enough.* And the truth was, at twenty years old, I wasn't exactly a saint myself. I drank more than I should, but I knew enough to stay away from the drug scene, something Jeff couldn't seem to do. When he turned eighteen, I helped him get a job in the mine where I worked. He would be on third shift, which meant most of his nights were occupied, cutting down on the time he could party. He and Kimberly got pregnant again, and their second daughter, Andrea, was born in July 1982. The camper became much too cramped for a family of four, so they bought a trailer and put it about a hundred yards down the road from where they had been living.

Jeff loved his girls with all his heart. I couldn't help but smile when I watched Jeff with them, holding them, beaming when he talked about them. His daughters brought out this amazing, caring, patient version of my brother – doctoring booboos and holding them to his chest, soothing their cries with whispered words. But on the weekends, he and Kimberly just couldn't stay home and play Mommy and Daddy. With two little girls, they couldn't go out, so they brought the parties to their trailer.

Mom, who had stayed relatively quiet through most of Jeff's wild excursions, stepped in at that point. She couldn't stand the thought of her granddaughters in that atmosphere. She told Jeff if he and Kimberly were going to have drugs in their home, she couldn't stop them, but she wasn't going to allow the girls to be in the middle of it. Jeff and Kim were all too happy to hand the girls over every weekend. Every Friday and Saturday night, the girls took turns staying with Mom and me, or Grandma. They were too young to understand what was going on at home, and they seemed to enjoy their time with us. I fell in love with those girls like they were my own.

Other than the weekend parties, things seemed to be going right in Jeff's life. He and Kimberly were happy, they had two beautiful daughters, and Jeff held down his job at the coal mine. When I married my girlfriend, Diane, we moved into a small house down the road. I switched to third shift, which allowed Jeff and me to ride to work together. At nine thirty each night, I picked him up. We laughed and joked like old times. I slept easier at night. My little brother was back.

But the peace didn't last long. Less than a year later, Jeff found out that when he left the house to go to work each night, his good friend Dave was sneaking through the woods to visit Kimberly. A vicious divorce followed, leaving Kimberly with custody of the girls and Jeff with weekend visitations. One weekend, when Jeff showed up to get them, he found Kimberly's house empty – she had packed up the girls and all their belongings and gone to Florida to live with some of her family.

This was a violation of the divorce decree and custody agreement. The girls, at only two and three years old, had no idea what was happening. Jeff immediately went to court and got a judge's order to bring his girls back home. We both used our vacation days as well as some sick days to fly to Florida to track them down. Mom and Dad both came along as well. While Mom hated the idea of traveling anywhere with Dad, she knew his badge could provide us with much-needed assistance when it came to finding her grandbabies. They managed to ignore each other as much as possible throughout the trip, which was the most civil I'd seen them in years.

Once we got there, we weren't sure where to go. All we knew was they would be somewhere near Sarasota. We rented a car and spent five days searching – calling relatives, leaving messages, driving to places we thought they might be – to no avail. Almost a week had passed without so much as a clue as to where they might be.

Out of days off from work, Jeff and I both knew we had to return home. The flight home was somber. Jeff sat next to me. He didn't speak and barely acknowledged my efforts to make small talk. His red-rimmed eyes sagged and though he didn't make a sound, a solitary tear fell down his cheek as the plane began its takeoff. He made plans to return the following weekend to continue his search.

As luck would have it, he caught a break as soon as we arrived home. Kimberly called him from a payphone, asking him to send money for child support.

Jeff wanted to scream at her, to demand that she bring the girls home right away. But somehow, he managed to stay calm and be smart about the situation. "I'll send you money," he promised. "But all I really want is to talk to the girls."

"They're not with me right now."

It was exactly the answer he hoped for. "That's okay. Could you bring them back to that payphone tomorrow night? Say, at seven o'clock? Give me the number, and I'll call it. I just need to hear their voices."

Kimberly agreed. Jeff hung up the phone and called the police, who tracked the number of the payphone she gave him. When she and the girls showed up the next evening at seven o'clock, the cops were waiting. They took the girls and put them in foster care for two days until Jeff and Mom could get a flight down to get them.

I went to St. Louis to meet them at the airport when they returned. I'd never been so happy to see their sweet little smiles, their curls bouncing as they ran to hug me. In their young minds, they'd simply been on a little vacation. They didn't understand what their mother had done, didn't understand the heartache and worry and stress their disappearance had caused for Jeff and our family. Even staying with a foster family had been an adventure – all they knew was their daddy was coming to get them soon.

Back home, a judge granted Jeff temporary custody prior to the hearing. Kimberly didn't even fight him for the girls. When the hearing rolled around, Jeff was awarded full custody while Kimberly stayed in Florida with her family.

The chaos of the situation diverted my attention away from the fact my own personal life as I knew it was falling apart – Diane and I, after only a year of marriage, realized we couldn't make our relationship work and decided to divorce. To distract myself from the failure I felt at the end of my marriage, I threw myself into work and helping Jeff raise his girls on his own. He and I became closer than ever and I loved every minute of watching those little girls grow up.

When Jeff met Abigail, they hit it off right away. She seemed to be a good fit for him – she supported him and took in those girls like they were hers. What I liked best about her was she was never much for the party scene, which I hoped would help Jeff stay on the right path. They got engaged after just a few months of dating, and while I couldn't have been happier for them, the wedding was a stressful event for our family. At the rehearsal dinner, as soon as Mom got within a few feet of Dad, she started an argument, creating a scene when the attention should have been on Jeff and Abigail. I spent the entire wedding and reception making sure my parents stayed separated to prevent it from happening again.

Soon after the wedding, I met Lori. Like Jeff when he met Abigail, I was smitten from the first date. We married in January 1986, and the following month, Jeff and Abigail welcomed their third daughter, Megan, to the world. Lori and I rented an apartment near Jeff and Abigail's house, which allowed me to see the girls every day. Jeff and I continued to ride to work together, but we also spent a lot of time together during the daytime hours, usually fishing or hunting. Jeff seemed to love family life and my worries over his wild days became no more than a distant memory.

I went to church with Lori, which wasn't out of the ordinary – we had been raised in church. But one Monday night at a revival when I was twenty-five years old, I found God in a way I never had before. Suddenly, all those Bible stories I'd heard growing up, the message of Jesus's love and sacrifice sank in, and I surrendered my heart to Him. Though I'd prayed with a preacher and been baptized when I was only ten years old, this was different. It was real. I wasn't going through the motions anymore – I was sold out for Jesus. I was forgiven, my old life washed away.

I was saved on Monday, and shot on Wednesday. While turkey hunting with Lori's brother, a stranger in the woods heard my call and saw movement. I heard the shotgun blast just moments before pellets pierced me from my fingertips to my shoulder, some mere inches from my heart, shooting pain through my chest and pulsing in the rest of my body. But by the grace of God, after a very brief recovery, I was okay. The person who shot me fled the scene and was never caught, but I had peace with it all. I knew God was watching over me that day.

I wanted so much for Jeff to experience what I had. We invited Jeff and Abigail and the girls to come to a Sunday morning church service with us. They began to attend regularly and seemed to enjoy it, though I knew for Jeff, his heart hadn't been softened to it the way mine had. He came almost out of obligation — it was the right thing for a man to do, bringing his family to church — but he didn't care to become too active in it. For a long time, my attitude had been similar, and I knew pushing him wasn't the way to handle it. I tried to stay in the background, watching as week after week, he and his family came to church and praying each Sunday it would be the day he let Jesus in.

Though he never had that *moment* like I had in that revival that night, I was still amazed by how far he'd come. He still smoked pot on occasion, but overall, he was a new man.

On January 23, 1987, I became a father myself. When our daughter, Tiffany, was born, I experienced a new and powerful love I'd never known. Jeff and Abigail bought a house out of town with a few acres and a big yard, and Lori and I moved into a new home just a few blocks away. Our families were always together. Jeff's girls loved their new home. We spent hours in that yard, Lori and I on a blanket with Tiffany as Jeff chased his girls around the yard while they toddled away, squealing in delight.

When deer season rolled around, Jeff and I became like kids all over again. I still found myself unable to sleep the night before opening day. The two of us would go out into the woods for three or four days at a time, staying in deer camps with our buddy, Stan, my brother-in-law, Terry, and my nephew, Troy. We laughed around camp fires, just like we did in our younger years.

It was at one of those deer camps when I noticed Jeff popping a few too many pain pills.

Chapter Five
Doctor Hopping

In 1989, I left Sahara Coal to go to work as a field service representative at Long-Airdox, a mining equipment manufacturing company. It wasn't a decision I made lightly – I enjoyed working with my brother and. valued our conversations as we rode together each night. But things were going so well for him, and I felt this was the right decision for my family.

Jeff, like many in the mines, sustained a couple minor injuries while working. He went to the doctor, described his pain, and was given a prescription for pain pills. His aches were legitimate, but he just couldn't seem to take those pills as directed – he always had to take an extra one. And when he combined those pain pills with a joint, he entered his favorite relaxed state of mind.

One night at deer camp, when we retired to our cabin for the night, I watched him take out a brand new prescription bottle and toss a few in his mouth.

I eyed the bottle. "What are those for?"

"Uh, I've had some pain in my neck." He shrugged. "You know how it is in the mines."

"Yeah, I guess." I crossed my arms. "I thought you just had some sort of pain pills for something else? Not too long ago? That looks like a new bottle."

"It is."

I nodded slowly. "Huh."

He stood up. "All right, you're thinking something – might as well come out and say it."

Frowning, I lifted one shoulder and let it drop. "I don't know. Just thinking…I'm sorta surprised Dr. Lowery would prescribe you more pain pills. Since he just gave you that other prescription, you know?"

Jeff rubbed the back of his neck. "Oh, uh, I didn't get these from Lowery. I went to Roberts."

I raised my eyebrows. "You switched doctors?"

"Um, no, I wouldn't say that, exactly. I'm sure I'll go back to Lowery again. I just…" He ducked his head, pretending to pick at some lint on his shirt.

And that's when the pieces fell into place in my mind. "You're doctor-hopping. Going around to different doctors and getting them to give you pain pills."

He chuckled. "Oh, don't say it like that. You make it sound like I'm doing something wrong. And I actually need these. Working underground…it ain't easy on the body."

I didn't say anything. What could I say? Back in those days, doctors didn't have computer systems to tie our records together. I knew he'd get away with it. But why? Things in his life seemed to be going so well. He was happy. Why did he feel the need to stay medicated like that?

Something churned in my stomach. "Jeff, I…" I couldn't find the words. There was so much I wanted to say, and yet I didn't know how. He was my best friend. We were closer than we'd ever been, even closer than we were as kids. As ridiculous as it seemed, I didn't want anything to mess that up. Maybe if I didn't really acknowledge it, the problem would go away.

"What?" He plopped down on his bed and stared at me, something in his eyes almost daring me to start an argument.

I sighed. "Just be careful, okay?"

He smirked. "Don't worry, big brother. I'll be fine."

I watched him closely through the rest of our time at deer camp. Every time he had a beer or two, he snuck a small handful of pills at the same time. My stomach sank. Something in the back of my mind whispered that his perfect life may be in danger of falling apart, but again, I silenced that voice. *He's got a good life. He won't mess that up.*

My new job required travel, making it difficult to keep a close eye on him. Then, on April 5, 1991, my son, Jackson, was born. Between work and caring for my growing family, I couldn't follow my brother's every move the way I'd done in the past. But when I was with him, he seemed his usual, happy self. He took his girls fishing. He took them to the woods to scout for deer and put up tree stands. He and Abigail never missed a school play or a softball game. He was still the loving, attentive dad and husband I respected him for being.

But one day out of the blue, I got a call from our good buddy, Stan. Stan and Jeff had remained close even as they grew older. Stan had retired from their mischievous pranks they were so infamous for as kids, even becoming a youth pastor after graduating high school. Though several of the other neighborhood boys had moved away or lost touch with us, Stan was the one constant in our lives. He looked out for Jeff like I did, like a brother.

"Hey, Stan. What's going on?"

"Uh, not much. It's just...something kinda weird happened today. Wanted to hear your thoughts on it."

"All right. Everything okay?"

"Yeah, it's...it's fine, I guess, I just...well, Jeff and I went to RadioShack today, looking for one of those voice-activated recorders to use for turkey hunting."

"Oh, yeah? You get one?" Nothing seemed out of the ordinary yet – Jeff had mentioned wanting one before.

"Well, that's the thing. There was this young salesman in there, helping us. Jeff had him get out every one of those recorders they had. He'd have him get one out, and he'd look it over really good, then have him put that one up and get out another one. He inspected each one of those things like he was buying a car."

I laughed. "I never knew he was so particular about a recorder."

Stan sighed. "So, we ended up leaving the store without making any kind of decision. But then, we got in my truck, pulled out of the parking lot and started down the road, and then...Jeff pulled one out of his pocket."

My heart raced as Stan's words sank in. "You mean...he stole one?"

"Yeah. And the thing was, he laughed about it. Like it was some kind of a game. He didn't see anything wrong with what he did."

I closed my eyes, feeling sick to my stomach. I remembered his theft habit when he was a teen, but I thought his days of that were long behind him. Why would he need to steal? He made good money in the coal mine. Abigail had a beauty shop in town where she had many loyal customers. He was in the best financial state he'd ever been.

Stan echoed my thoughts. "Any idea why he'd do that?"

"No," I admitted. "I'm not sure what's going on with him these days."

But before I could talk to my brother about it, something happened to distract us all. A few coal mines in southern Illinois started going out of business, and in 1993, Sahara Coal followed suit. Jeff found himself without a job.

Dad and I were still close, and though he and Jeff had a rocky history, at that point, the two were closer than I'd ever seen them. But I had to admit, I was a little surprised when the three of us sat together in Jeff's living room one day and Dad said, "There's a job opening I think you should apply for."

Jeff looked up from the TV. "What is it?"

"A correctional officer. Saline County Detention Center."

A little snort escaped my mouth, but they both ignored me. Jeff tilted his head. "What qualifications do I need?"

"Well, you'll have to get through training at the Academy. And you'll have to pass a test. You interested?"

Jeff's eyes narrowed as he seemed to consider it. "Yeah," he said finally. "I think I am."

My jaw dropped. It wasn't that I didn't think Jeff could do the job – I knew he could do whatever he put his mind to. But he wanted to? That was what surprised me. *He won't really go through with this. Will he?*

He did. He made it through six weeks of training at the academy, then took the test and passed it. He had pushed himself physically and mentally, and it paid off – Jeff got the job.

I called him at the end of his first day. "Well? How was it?"

"You know what? I think I'm going to like it."

"Really? That's great, Jeff. I'm really proud of you. This is a good thing. For you and your family."

"Yeah. And you know, I was thinking…I might even like to

become a deputy. Eventually, anyway."

I almost fell out of my chair. "Wow. That's...that's wonderful." The irony of the situation wasn't lost on me – Jeff, who spent the first part of his life resisting authority and bucking the system whenever he could, suddenly wanted to be on the other side of the law. But I embraced his new lifestyle. "I'm proud of you," I told him again.

With each passing week, he seemed to love the job more. He mentioned the sheriff's deputy goal more than once. My worries from the months before eased. *He won't break the law anymore...he* is *the law.*

But after just a year and a half at the Detention Center, Jeff lost his job. He refused to talk about it with anyone, but through Dad's connections, we learned the gist of the situation. It seemed Jeff had been allowing a male inmate access to female cells, though the details were vague. Was it a guy visiting his girl-friend? We never found out the whole story. All we knew was, whatever the situation, it cost him his job.

I could see how crushed he was to lose that position. He was back to square one – no job, and no real prospects. So when I heard Long-Airdox had an opening, I called Jeff immediately. "Hey, we're hiring. It's a warehouse position. You'd be pulling parts, loading trucks, and then driving to different mines to sup-ply them. You better come up here and apply."

I could hear his sigh of relief on the other end. "I'm on my way."

He got the job. My brother and I would be working together again.

For the first couple weeks, things seemed great. He charmed everyone at Long-Airdox with his friendly personality and fun-ny stories. But being around him all the time meant that once again, I saw his every move. And that included the pain pills he continued to sneak when he thought no one was looking.

Things really fell apart one weekend when Abigail found a bag of pot stashed in his truck. He had kept his recreational smoking habits from her all that time, and she was furious. For Abigail, that was the final straw, all she needed to kick him out of the house – I learned soon after that the two were already having problems, though Jeff hadn't shared that with me.

They still owned their first house they had in town, so Jeff moved back into it. And before I knew what had even happened, things really spun out of control, like a toilet flushing, and I just couldn't get my foot in to stop it.

Chapter Six
Wrestling To Rehab

Things began turning up missing at work. Small things, like a laptop. A few pieces of cable that could be sold for the copper inside. A pistol disappeared from someone's drawer.

My boss accused the cleaning crew, but something in the back of my mind told me exactly who the culprit was. I just didn't want to believe it. Sure, my brother had stolen some things through the years. But from the company he works for? The company where I got him a job? Talk about a slap in my face. He *couldn't* have. He wouldn't jeopardize his career like that, wouldn't risk his or my reputation by doing something so foolish.

Yet it had his name all over it. The thefts, the way the items went missing – it was exactly his mode of operation. It was how he worked as a teen: steal something people wouldn't notice for a little while, and by the time they did, there'd be no way to find the thief.

He started missing work. Once a month quickly turned into once a week.

Around this time, Grandma developed Alzheimer's and had to move in with Mom. Jeff moved into her house and rented out the house in town he had lived in. He started a relationship with a much-younger girlfriend – a girl I didn't know well, though I knew her father – and she moved in to Grandma's house, too.

I knew something was going on, something more serious than smoking a little pot or taking some extra pain pills. I confronted him. "Jeff, is there something I need to know?"

He laughed and shook his head. "Why do you always do this?"

"Do what?"

"Try to make a big deal out of nothing. I'm fine. Sure, I've hit a little rough patch. But I'll come through it. I always do."

I squared my shoulders and looked him straight in the eye. "Are you on drugs? And I'm not talking about a little weed or a few painkillers."

He looked up at the sky in exasperation. "Okay, Jack, you're being ridiculous. This conversation is over."

But it wasn't over for me. I knew there was something he wasn't telling me. I spent my nights tossing and turning, worrying, imagining where he might be or what he might be doing. When I slept, I had nightmares about it.

Driving by his house every day gave me my first clue: I spotted the same red truck in his driveway twice in the same week. Asking around town, I learned who the truck belonged to – a guy in town I suspected used drugs. When he was busted a week later for selling, my suspicions were confirmed.

I went to Dad. "Dad, I…I think Jeff is getting in over his head. He's missing work, stealing. He's hanging out with some…bad people."

Dad sighed. "I know."

I raised my eyebrows. "You do?"

"Yeah." He dropped his gaze and started to pace. "I've known something was going on. I started talking to people a few days ago, seeing what I could find out."

I'd always half-joked about Dad and his network of snitches. Growing up, we couldn't get away with anything without him finding out what we'd done before we ever got home. He even knew about the infamous oil barrel incident, though he never asked us about it – I think he figured the less he knew, the better.

But for the first time in my life, I was grateful for Dad's connections. "Well? What'd you hear?"

Dad rubbed his fingers back and forth across his forehead, as if he had a headache. "I'm afraid he's gotten into crack cocaine."

My throat went dry. *Crack cocaine?*

My whole life, I had felt this urge to protect my little brother. But now, watching over him became an obsession. I kept a close eye on him, driving by Grandma's house and trying to monitor where he was and who he was with at all times.

I drove by one evening and noticed he and his girlfriend

weren't there. On impulse, I whipped in the driveway, got out of the car, and let myself inside. I walked around, looking for any evidence of Dad's allegation while desperately hoping I wouldn't find anything. And I didn't. The house was relatively clean. But when I looked up at the mantle, I noticed some of the antiques Grandma kept on display there were missing. At first I didn't think much of it. *Maybe the new girlfriend doesn't like that style of decoration.* But the more I walked around the house, the more I noticed had disappeared. Grandma had a lot of really valuable antiques, and I couldn't find one of them. My stomach churned. *He wouldn't. Not from Grandma. Maybe he stole from work, but he wouldn't steal from her.*

But again, I knew. Where else would he get the money for an expensive habit like crack cocaine?

He didn't show up for work the next day. My boss didn't even try to hide the irritation on his face any longer. "Jack, you know where Jeff's at today?"

I sucked in a breath, searching for any excuse I could give for him. But something inside of me whispered, *tell him the truth.* And that's exactly what I did. I told him how his marriage had fallen apart, how he'd gotten involved in a rough crowd since he moved out of the house he shared with Abigail and the girls. I even told him about the missing antiques.

He listened, his face solemn. When I finished my story, he shook his head. "I'm sorry to hear all that. And I'm sorry you're going through this, Jack."

I nodded. "I'm sorry to put you in this position. I wanted you to hire him, and now…"

He held up his hands. "Hey, none of this is your fault."

I didn't tell him that I couldn't help but feel some responsibility, though I knew it was crazy. "If it's okay with you, sir, I think I'll take off early today. It's time to confront him. Get him some help before this gets out of hand."

He clasped my shoulder. "Do what you need to do."

When I left, I made two phone calls. First, I called Stan and told him I was coming to pick him up. I knew I couldn't stage an intervention by myself, and I figured if Stan was with me, he might be a little more willing to listen. Next, I called the father of Jeff's girlfriend. When I told him a little bit of what was going on, he confirmed that he and his wife suspected the same thing about their daughter. He had already contemplated going over to Grandma's house and dragging her out of there, and my phone call was all he needed to decide to go through with it.

When Stan and I pulled into the driveway, Jeff was there. His girlfriend was already gone. I shut off my truck and just sat there, staring at the house.

"You ready for this?" Stan asked, his voice almost a whisper.

I sighed. "No."

"Me neither."

I got out of the truck, my heart leaping into my throat. I took a deep breath and pulled myself up to my full height. If I didn't feel confident, at least I could try to look it.

We walked inside to find Jeff at the dining room table, though the table was empty. No surprise registered on his face at our presence. The defiant look in his eyes told me he knew what we were there for.

I pulled up a chair next to him and Stan lowered himself into the one on his other side. I gave him a long, hard look. "We need to talk, little brother."

Jeff's eyes narrowed. "If you're here for the reason I think you are, we've got nothing to talk about."

Stan and I looked at each other. He gave me a single nod of encouragement.

"I know what you've been up to. Don't even try to keep lying to me about it – I'm not leaving 'til you admit the truth. I'll sit here all night if I have to."

Jeff leaned back in his chair and crossed his arms over his chest, a small smirk playing on the corners of his lips. "That'd be fine with me."

Stan put his elbows on the table and leaned forward. "Buddy, we're here because we care about you. We're your best friends." He sighed. "Come on, you used to tell me everything. What's going on?"

Jeff's face fell. His lips twitched, but he still said nothing.

"It's true, isn't it?" I kept my voice low and even. "You're using crack cocaine?"

42

Jeff's eyes darted to mine. He opened his mouth, closed it, then opened it again. "So what if I am?"

My chest seemed to deflate. I knew it was true, but hearing him admit it still crushed me into a million pieces. "Jeff, you can't...it's ruining your life. Can't you see that?"

That cocky smirk reappeared. "Oh, don't be so dramatic, Jack."

I raised my eyebrows. "Dramatic? Jeff, you lost your wife. You're not seeing your girls as much as you should be. You're skipping out on work –"

"What, are you spying on me?" Anger flashed in his eyes.

I sat up straighter in my chair. "What if I am?"

When Jeff stood to his feet, knocking his chair backward, Stan stood up, too. He raised his hands. "Easy, Jeff. He's only looking out for you because he loves you. We both love you."

Jeff swallowed. His clenched fists relaxed, and he lowered himself back into his chair.

I eased my hand forward until it rested on his arm. He flinched, but didn't move. I took that as my sign to continue. "You're playing with fire. And we don't want to see you get burned. Where did you...how did you even get started in that stuff, anyway? Where'd you get the money to –"

"That's none of your business."

Despite his raised tone, I kept my calm. "It is my business when you're selling Grandma's antiques for drugs."

His jaw dropped, and I was sure he was about to object, but to my surprise, he didn't. His eyes searched mine for a moment before he said, "I didn't sell them. Well, not all of them."

"Then where did they go?"

"I put them up somewhere."

It was a lie, and we both knew it. I shook my head. "Then where are you getting the money? I know it's not a cheap habit to have."

His eyes dropped to the table. "I...I took out my 401K from Sahara."

I stared at him. "How much of it have you used?"

"Not all of it." He crossed his arms, indignant. "There's still some left."

"Some?" I put my fingers to my temples. "Jeff, what are you thinking? Blowing through your savings on drugs? That money...you may really need it someday. Your girls may need it."

"How much are you spending?" Stan's voice surprised us both. We turned and looked at him. He tilted his head. "How much is this little habit of yours costing?"

I never expected him to answer. He gazed at Stan, seemingly considering the question, before he let out a deep sigh. "About a hundred bucks a day."

For a moment, I wished we hadn't even come. I knew he had a problem, but with every new admission, I realized the severity of it all. My little brother was slipping through my fingers, and once again, I had no idea what to do about it.

But while every ounce of my body wanted to run away, to hide from it all and pretend it wasn't happening, I stood up and planted my feet. "You're going to get help. Stan and I are taking you to rehab. Today."

Jeff snorted. "I'm not going anywhere."

"Oh, yes, you are. You'll go if we have to drag you there, kicking and screaming."

And that's what we had to do, in a way. Jeff stood up, poised to run away, but I was faster. I tackled him to the ground before he could get out of the dining room. He fought back, but I had a strength I'd never had before, a determination that was stronger than any punch he threw.

For five hours, we wrestled in the middle of my Grandma's house. We'd fight until neither of us could breathe, then fall away from each other, staring at each other as we recovered. The match would resume. Stan stayed out of it as much as he could, intervening only when he thought one of us was about to get seriously hurt.

Finally, Jeff couldn't take anymore. He could see we weren't going anywhere. He bent over, resting his hands on his knees while he panted. "Fine. I'll go."

Stan and I looked at each other. I sighed in relief, too exhausted to say anything.

We drove him to the closest drug rehab center I knew of: The Mulberry Center in Evansville, about an hour away. Jeff didn't speak on the way there. He stared out the window, his chin jutted out in defiance though he'd admitted defeat. I didn't let the look of disdain on his face when we pulled into the parking lot deter me. *This is the right thing to do. I can't give him the help he needs – this is bigger than me. These people are professionals. They'll know how to counsel him, how to help him get his life back on track.*

Stan and I stood on either side of him while he checked himself in, supplying the receptionist with information when Jeff hesitated. He made it clear through his actions and facial expressions he didn't think it was necessary to be there. Admitting himself on a voluntary basis, there was no evidence he needed help, and I wondered what he would do or say when we left. I imagined him telling the nurses, "My brother is crazy. I don't have a problem. Would you just let me out of here so I can go home?"

No, he won't. He didn't let us bring him all this way for nothing. With their help, he'll kick this addiction, and we can all put this nightmare behind us.

When he was all checked in, I grabbed him and pulled him to my chest in a tight hug. Tears dripped down my cheeks. Our five-hour wrestling match was forgotten as he hugged me back, clutching my shirt under his fingers. "You can do this," I said through my tears. "You're one of the strongest people I know."

He didn't say anything. I wasn't sure how long we stood like that, holding each other. A minute? An hour? I didn't want to let him go, though I knew I had to.

When we finally pulled away from each other, Stan embraced him. "Get better, buddy. We'll see you soon, okay?"

Again, Jeff didn't respond.

The look on his face when Stan and I walked away is an image that will forever be etched into my brain. The wild defiance in his eyes was gone, replaced by a wounded fear I didn't recognize in my brother. I had to tell myself to put one foot in front of the other, to drag myself away from him and leave him in the care of the Mulberry Center. It went against every brotherly instinct in my body. I was his keeper, his protector. Why couldn't I fix this? Left on his own with the professionals, would he do what he needed to do to fix it himself?

Walking out those doors was one of the hardest moments of my life to that point. *You have to do this. You* have *to.* But saying those words in my mind over and over didn't ease the pain of it. I got in my truck, the image of Jeff's face still burning in my mind. Stan's presence beside me, knowing he felt the same pain I felt at that moment, gave me enough comfort to pull myself together. I wiped the fresh tears from my cheeks and drove away, leaving my little brother behind.

Chapter Seven
Recovering The Missing

The Mulberry Center program is thirty days by design. But three weeks after Stan and I took Jeff there, he checked himself out. With his admission there being voluntary and not enforced by a court order, he was free to do so.

My heart pounded when he called me to come get him. "Jeff, you're almost done with the program. Nine more days. Can't you just finish it out?"

His irritated sigh echoed in my ear. "Jack, please. I can't be here any longer. I don't need to be here. I've got it together now, I promise. I...I need to be home with my family. My girls need me."

Something leapt around in my stomach during the hour-long drive to pick him up. *What if it wasn't long enough? What if he comes home and falls right back into that life?*

I shook my head. *This is Jeff you're talking about. Your little brother. He's not destined for that life — we weren't raised that way. It'll be okay now. Those three weeks were enough for him to clear his mind, get his head on straight.*

He waited outside for me when I pulled into the parking lot. As soon as he saw my truck, he stood from the bench and threw his bag over his shoulder. As I got closer, a wide grin spread over his face. My racing heart slowed. *He looks good. Better than I've seen him in a while.*

The more we talked on the way home, the more my nerves relaxed. He talked about what he would do when he got home, about picking up his girls and taking them fishing. He laughed about old times and looked forward to deer camp in a couple months. I laughed along with him and sighed in relief on the inside. *My brother is back. Everything is going to be okay.*

But if you come back home and get mixed up with the same people, things will go right back to how they were before you left. Unfortunately, that's exactly what Jeff did.

I didn't see it at first. Or maybe I just didn't want to see it. When I drove up to the corner by his house and spotted a truck I thought I recognized – someone known for drug use – I turned the other direction. *You're being paranoid. That's not who that was. It was probably just one of the girls' friends. He's done with that.* I knew better, even as I rationalized it in my mind. But something inside of me wouldn't allow me to admit the truth. He *couldn't* be using again. If he was, what were those three weeks for? Those hours of wrestling before we finally convinced him to get help? Was it all for nothing?

He came back to Long-Airdox and worked the midnight shift, getting the trucks ready for delivery in the morning and making emergency runs through the night. He often drove a company vehicle. One morning, when Christina was staying with him and had a friend visiting, he backed into her friend's car and did considerable damage to the company's truck.

Human Resources, knowing his past, was put on alert. It wasn't long after that items began to turn up missing in the office again. And when he left work one morning, he fell asleep while driving, totaled his personal vehicle, and ended up in the hospital. He would be okay, but had to stay there for a couple days to recover.

The State Police ordered a drug test. HR asked for the results of that test as well.

I knew I couldn't jeopardize the company any longer by pretending Jeff was okay. When I got off work that day, I drove to the hospital clutching a resignation slip in my hand. I made my way to Jeff's room, resolved to do what I knew I had to do. I barely even greeted him before I looked him in the eye and held out that slip. "Jeff, you've got to quit."

He flinched. "Quit?"

I shoved the paper at him. "If you don't, you'll be fired. HR… they're onto you. The missing stuff, the accidents…"

He stared at me. I held my head high, prepared for an argument. After all, they didn't have proof yet. In Jeff's eyes, that meant he was innocent.

But he didn't even try to deny it. He nodded once. "Okay. I'll sign it."

I faxed the signed papers to Long-Airdox as soon as I got home. Then I got into the car and drove to our grandmother's house, not allowing myself to think about Jeff and the problems that were bound to continue and likely get worse since he found himself once again without a job. Instead, I kept my focus on my mission: I was going to find the items he'd stolen from the company.

I parked my car in the driveway and let myself in the house. An invisible weight pressed on my chest. *You're a failure,* a little voice in my mind whispered. *You let this happen. You didn't protect Jeff, and you didn't protect the company. You failed them both.*

I shook my head, trying to chase that voice away. *Focus. Do what you came here to do.*

I combed every inch of the house, recovering a few of the missing items – a laptop, some pieces of cable. It wasn't everything, but I knew the rest of it was long gone, traded for drugs. I loaded the things I did find in my truck to return to my boss the next day.

My boss was a compassionate man – I saw that a few weeks earlier when I told him about Jeff's struggles – and I knew the best route I could take was to simply tell him the truth once again. I gave him the items I had found along with a difficult and heartfelt apology. "Thank you for being so understanding. But I'm afraid...he hasn't worked through his problems just yet. I didn't...I shouldn't have asked you to...to take a chance on him." I sighed. "I know you have to do what you have to do. I just...I hope there's no hard feelings. Between us, I mean."

He sucked in a deep breath and held it in his cheeks before letting it trickle out. "I'm so sorry, Jack. I appreciate your efforts. And your honesty." He tilted his head. "I hope you realize I don't hold any of this against you."

I nodded. "I appreciate that, sir." But I still couldn't help feeling responsible.

Long-Airdox ultimately decided not to prosecute. But a couple days later, while Jeff was still in the hospital, I got a call from

Stan.

"Hey, buddy. How are you?" I leaned back in my recliner and did my best to sound upbeat when I greeted him. I was always happy to hear from Stan, but after two days of beating myself up and worrying about Jeff and his future, I was struggling. Sometimes I felt like I lived in this little bubble of pain and anxiety no one else could see. At least Stan lived there with me.

I knew something was wrong when I heard his breath catch on the other end. "Hey, Jack."

"What's wrong?"

There was a long pause before he sighed. "I...I'm afraid my business is in trouble."

I frowned. Stan had a Rent-to-Own business in Harrisburg – a business that, from what he'd last told me, was doing pretty well. "In trouble? What do you mean?"

"Well, I think...I've had..." He sighed again. "Some of my stuff, it's..."

My heart sank. I knew somehow before he said another word where this conversation was going. "He's been stealing from you." It wasn't a question.

Another pause. "Well, I don't know that for sure, but..."

"What's missing?"

"Some TVs. VCRs. Stereos."

I sighed. "How did he...did he break in?"

"No, not break in. I...he has a key, Jack."

I raised my eyebrows. "A key?"

"He talked me into giving him one, back when he was making those night deliveries for Long-Airdox."

I sighed. "Oh, Stan."

"I know, I know. But...he said...when he was out through the night, he needed a place to stop. You know, for bathroom breaks. I didn't think twice about making him one, honestly, but then...at first I thought it was one of my employees. And I mean, it could be, I guess."

"It's him, Stan. You know it is."

Another long pause. "If I don't recover some of that stuff, my business will be in jeopardy."

I closed my eyes. Part of me wanted to scold him. *What were you thinking, giving a known drug addict and thief a key to your business?* But I didn't. Truth was, I figured I probably would have done the same. Stan wanted to trust Jeff, to believe he was turning his life around, just as much as I did. "I'm sorry, Stan."

"It's not your fault. I just…I didn't know who else to call." He sighed. "I shouldn't have even bothered you with this. I'm sure that stuff is long-gone by now. There's nothing either of us can do about it."

"No, I'm glad you called me." As I said those words, a wild idea came to mind. "What if…what if there *was* something we could do about it?"

I pictured Stan's eyes narrowing as he considered my question. "Like what?"

I swallowed. My heart raced as the idea grew. "Well…you and I both know he traded that stuff for drugs. Just like Grandma's antiques." I leaned forward, my head spinning with frustration. Stealing from our grandmother was bad enough, but stealing from his best friend? I couldn't just sit back and watch Stan's business fall apart at the hands of my brother. "What if…what if we found out who was supplying him, and we went to them and demanded your stuff back?"

Stan snorted. "Are you insane? Jack, you can't just show up at a drug dealer's house and make demands."

But the idea was still growing, taking anchor in my mind so that I barely heard him. I jumped out of my recliner and paced the length of the living room. "I think we can pull this off. In fact, I *know* we can." I planted my feet in the middle of the floor. "We're gonna get your stuff back. I promise."

My Brother's Keeper

My Brother's Keeper

Chapter Eight
A Wild Idea

Dad had retired from the Illinois State Police after thirty-two years of service. We all knew he wouldn't sit still for long, and soon after, he was elected as Saline County Circuit Clerk. Working there, he was still very much in the know of the court system, plus he still talked to his friends in law enforcement on a regular basis. I knew we could go to him to find out where to start our research.

Between Dad's informants and a few of Jeff's contacts I reached out to, it wasn't long before we had several names. We got the most information on a dealer named Donald, including his address and phone number. We also found out he'd taken some antiques on trade for drugs, and though I didn't know for sure, I was willing to bet money those antiques were the ones from my grandmother's house.

Another name was tossed out by different sources, though it was a just a nickname – Locust. No one seemed to know his real name or phone number, but we did manage to get an address and confirmation that he'd taken multiple electronic devices as drug trade. They had to be Stan's – they just *had* to be. We knew that's where we had to start.

"So what now?" I stood in the middle of Stan's living room on a Saturday afternoon, just three days after the conversation that sparked this wild, seemingly far-fetched idea that was quickly becoming a reality. "Do we call this Donald guy up? Tell him who we are and what we're after?"

"Maybe." Stan leaned forward in the recliner and rested his elbows on his knees. "Or maybe…I don't know. Maybe we need to check them all out a little further. You know, go by their places a few times. Stake them out. See what we're dealing with."

I raised my eyebrows. "They're drug dealers, Stan. I think we know what we're dealing with."

He rubbed the back of his neck and sighed. "You're right. We can't afford to wait too long. If my stuff is still there, I need to get it now before it gets traded off again and I lose it for good."

I nodded. "I think we need to start with Locust. We'll go tonight. We can park nearby, stake it out like you said. See how many people drop in. See what his peak hours of business are. If it's like I'm told, he'll work steadily through the night, but things will taper off when the sun comes up."

"That makes sense." Stan sighed. "Guess people would rather do this sort of business when it's dark and no one's out."

"The next night, we'll make our move. Or, actually, the following morning. Early. If he's been working all night, we can catch him at the end of his 'shift.' He'll be tired. Caught off-guard."

Stan's eyes narrowed as he considered the idea. "You're right." He nodded slowly. "I think that's the best way to do it. No warning, no unwanted guests in his place to back him up. You know, in case he decides to put up a fight."

I knew I couldn't do anything without talking to Lori first. I waited throughout the afternoon and evening for the right moment to tell her what Stan and I intended to do. I didn't want the kids to know. When I found her alone in the kitchen after dinner, cleaning up the dishes, I took a deep breath. *Here's your chance.*

"Hey, I need to tell you something."

She looked up at me, then lowered the plate in her hands back into the sink. "What is it?"

"I...I'm gonna go out for a bit tonight. With Stan."

Her eyebrows shot up. "Go out?"

"Yeah. It's..." I sighed. *Just tell her the truth.* "You know how Jeff stole that stuff from Stan? We...sort of think that we... might know where it is."

"Really?" She grabbed the towel next to the sink and dried her hands. "Where?"

"We're pretty sure the merchandise was traded for drugs."

The look Lori gave me said, *I could have told you that.*

"We got the name of the guy it was traded to. We're gonna get it back before he trades it off to somewhere else."

Lori turned slowly to face me. "What do you mean, you're 'gonna get it back'?"

"We're going over there. We've got the serial numbers of the merchandise. We'll go inside and search his place."

"With the police." She searched my face. When I hesitated, she shook her head. "No. Are you insane? You can't just...go to some drug dealer's house and do something like this."

"Yes, we can. Lori, I...you have to trust me. I know what I'm doing. I grew up watching my dad do this kind of stuff, remember?"

"Yeah, and your dad was a trained police officer, Jack!" She shifted, twisting the towel in her hands. "Do you think he would approve of something like this? Do you think he'd actually... *encourage* you to do something so dangerous?"

I leaned forward so my face was inches from hers. "Where do you think I got this guy's address? How do you think I know who these guys are in the first place?"

Lori stared at me. "So he knows about this?"

I nodded.

"And he is okay with it?"

"If he thought it was too dangerous, he'd never have agreed to help us." I reached forward to take the towel and laid it on the counter. I took her hands in mine. "Listen, we're not doing anything tonight. We just want to drive over there, stake it out a bit. See what we'll be dealing with. Then, the next night, we'll go back and make our move." I squeezed her hands. "I won't be stupid, Lori. You think I'd do something like this if I wasn't sure it would all turn out okay? You think I'd put myself in danger?"

She swallowed. "I just don't understand why you have to do this."

"Stan's business is in trouble, Lori."

"Yeah, because of Jeff. Not because of you." She sighed. "I know you feel this...this need to...clean up after him. But... don't you think this is going a little too far?"

She was right – I did hold myself responsible for fixing what he'd done. And I knew how ridiculous that must seem in her eyes. But I couldn't explain it. I had to do this. "I need you to trust me."

From the other side of the house, Tiffany shrieked with laughter. Jackson's muffled voice shouted, "Hey, give that back!"

Lori's head turned toward our kids. "Don't tell them what you're doing. They'll be scared to death."

"I didn't intend to." I squeezed her hands before I let go. "I'll leave after they go to bed. They won't even know I'm gone."

"Be careful, Jack. If something happened to you..."

"I will." I pulled her in and hugged her to me. "Thank you for understanding."

A couple hours later, dressed in dark clothes and a baseball cap, I headed out the door to begin our mission. Stan waited outside when I pulled up to get him. The two of us laughed and joked as we drove to the address I'd scrawled on a piece of paper, acting as though we were heading out to a ball game instead of a stakeout. A familiar bubble bounced around in my stomach – the same feeling I'd get when we were kids, toting buckets of corn kernels. Only now we weren't kids, and we weren't out looking for some innocent mischief. I didn't let myself worry, though, or really think about the danger of the situation. Not yet.

The apartment building rested on the end of a dead-end street. I turned the corner so that we faced it and pulled over before we got close. The street was dark except for a dim lamp at the end of it, shining light on about half the building. I shut off my headlights.

Stan and I stared in silence at the old, run-down building. Chipped paint decorated the outside. Overgrown shrubs served as the landscaping in front of the building. I squinted to make out a set of stairs that ran outside from the middle of the first floor to the second. I knew Locust's apartment was on that second floor. From what I could see, there wasn't much sign of life anywhere in the building. I sighed, wondering if Stan and I were wasting our time. I could be home. With my family. In my comfortable bed, getting some sleep before a full day of work tomorrow. What was I doing here?

As I thought about it, headlights flashed in my rearview mirror. Stan and I ducked automatically at the sight of the car turning the corner behind us. I watched out of the corner of my eye as a little black car went past us, the driver not giving us so much as a passing glance. It made its way down the street and came to a stop in front of the apartments, just past the point where the street lamp stopping shining on the building. A man jumped out of the car and took the outside steps two at a time, disappearing on the second floor. A few minutes later, he reappeared. He came back down the steps just as quickly as he'd gone up them, got back into the car, and started toward us. We ducked out of sight again until he was past us.

"That didn't take long," Stan said.

I smirked. "What didn't? That drug deal? Or were you talking about how long we had to sit here before we saw one happen?"

"Both."

We watched for hours as a steady flow of cars came down the dead-end street, all of them repeating the same pattern we'd seen with the first one. Some of those vehicles were exactly what I imagined Locust's "customers" would drive – cars that sputtered down the street and made you wonder if they'd even start again after being shut off. Others were exactly the opposite – nice, well-kept vehicles containing people who didn't look like they belonged in this part of town. Drugs were an equalizer, their effects the same on all types of people, their power reaching those from all walks of life.

My eyes grew heavy as the night went on. Beside me, Stan's head fell back against the headrest. I sighed. "You seen enough, buddy?"

"Yep."

I nodded. "Me too. I'm thoroughly disgusted enough for one night. Guess we'll go home and get a little rest so we're ready to come back tomorrow."

"You still want to?"

I started the truck without turning on the headlights and backed out of the spot we'd been sitting for the past several hours. "I don't see why not. Seems easy enough, right? We'll just sit out here and wait until all these people are gone. Just when his business is closed for the night, we'll surprise him. No big deal."

Stan nodded. "Okay. If you're sure about this."

"You want your stuff back, don't ya?"

"Yeah."

I ignored my lurching stomach and gave Stan a weak smile. "Then we're gonna get it back. Tomorrow." In my head, I added, *Lord, please be with us.*

Chapter Nine
Confronting The Darkness

So that's how, at six thirty the following morning, I found myself standing outside the apartment complex of the mysterious man called Locust, tucking a gun into the waist of my jeans. I pushed my shoulders back as I walked up the sidewalk toward the building, trying to project an air of confidence, but on the inside, I was shaking.

We saw the steady string of clients that came and visited Locust throughout the night. A source had told us that though he was one of the biggest suppliers of crack cocaine in the area, he didn't do it himself. He was smart enough to know how easy it was to become addicted and knew firsthand how much money it cost to keep up the habit. But I also figured that meant he was smart enough to have a gun or some sort of weapon for protection in the house. Drug dealers are often known for paranoia, and rightfully so, with the amount of money they exchange illegally on a daily basis. What would happen when we approached his door? Would he even answer it? Would he pull a gun on us? Would he let us in, only to harm us when we went inside?

Those questions swirled in my mind as I raised my fist to knock on his door. Again, I pictured Jeff's face. I imagined him climbing those same steps Stan and I had just climbed, pictured him carrying our grandmother's antiques or one of Stan's stereos in a desperate attempt to satisfy a craving that would never be truly satisfied. That's what it had come to? My baby brother was so engulfed in this downward spiral he'd steal from his family, his best friend, just to stay high for a few more hours? He didn't belong in this rundown apartment building, didn't belong among the other addicts who visited Locust in the middle of the night.

An image of my children – sound asleep in their beds, oblivious to the fact that their dad was standing at the door of a drug dealer – flashed through my mind. What was I doing here? How did we get here? Tears welled in my eyes until my hand shook and for a split second, I lowered it and considered abandoning our mission.

But I couldn't. We'd come too far. Because of my brother's actions, Stan's business was falling apart. Our family was falling apart. If I could do this one thing, if I could get back at least some of the missing stuff, I felt I could somehow get back a part of what was missing inside of me, too. Like this one little fix could be the beginning of a greater repair that would bring my old life, my old world, back to where it should be. With so much spinning out of my grasp, this seemed to be one thing I could actually take control of.

So I knocked. Three forceful raps in the middle of the door. Beside me, Stan sucked in a breath.

Silence. I waited about thirty seconds, then pounded on the door again, a little louder this time.

Silence again. Just as I raised my fist, prepared to knock a third time, I heard shuffling on the other side of the door. "Yeah?" a low, muffled voice called.

I swallowed. "Locust?"

Pause. "Who is this?"

Stan and I exchanged glances. "My name's Jack. I believe you know my brother, Jeff."

His voice was closer this time, and I could tell he was right behind the door. "What do you want?"

"I want to come inside. Talk to you for a minute. Why don't you open the door?"

After a moment of hesitation, the door knob turned. He pulled it open just a few inches, only as far as the chain lock allowed him to. "This is not a good time."

I stared into his cloudy eyes, and somewhere deep in my chest, something boiled. I was overcome by a strength, a confidence I knew didn't come from me, but from above. I no longer feared this stranger; my fear was replaced by anger. I knew my brother's habits were not Locust's fault, but at that moment, I blamed him for all the problems Jeff's addiction had caused in our family.

I cleared my throat. "I think it's a perfect time. You better open this door and let us in. I believe you have some things that belong to us."

He let out a sarcastic chuckle. A little spray of spit came out with it, narrowly missing my face. "I don't have nothing of yours."

I crossed my arms over my chest. "We can do this two ways. You can let us in now, or we can call the police. Let them know you have goods that were stolen from us that you've taken in exchange for drugs."

He stared at me. His mouth opened, but no sound came out.

I took advantage of his momentary speechlessness. "Look, we only want what's been stolen from us. We've got serial numbers of the electronics you've taken. Those are the ones we want. If you let us in, let us take back what's ours, we won't go to the police. You won't see us again."

His eyes cut into me. He closed the door, and for a moment, I was sure he was slamming the door in our faces. But then I heard the chain slide and the door seemed to open by itself. It creaked as it moved, inch-by-inch. What was he doing behind the door? Did he have a gun? Was he holding a baseball bat or some other weapon, ready to knock us over our heads as soon as we entered? My fingers moved automatically to my waistband. I was suddenly more aware of the cold steel pressed against my stomach. I curled my fingers around the gun, my heart racing until it pulsed in my throat and ears, and I took a step inside with Stan on my heels.

There wasn't a single light on inside the apartment. My eyes were wide as they adjusted to the darkness, darting immediately behind the door to lock in on Locust. I was surprised to find his hands empty, but I didn't let myself relax. His eyes narrowed as he assessed first me and then Stan.

"Where are they?" I held my chin in the air, still trying to maintain that air of confidence.

He shrugged and gestured behind us.

I glanced back. The apartment was pitch-black except for a sliver of light that came in through the small gap in the dark curtains. I could vaguely make out the outlines of various items scattered along the edge of the small living room. I was sure I could make out at least one television, though I was too scared to keep my eyes off Locust for more than a few seconds so I couldn't be sure.

I gave Stan a nod. "Go look through that stuff. I'll wait here." Stan looked at Locust, who didn't say a word, then back at me. He pulled a small piece of paper from his back pocket and opened it up. "I've got those serial numbers right here. I only want what's been stolen from my store."

Locust remained mute. Stan studied him for just a moment before he turned around and stepped toward the other side of the room. I was tempted to ask him to turn on a light, but decided against it. It would make it easier for Stan to read the barcodes that way, but it would also allow Locust to get a good look at our faces, too.

I kept my eyes locked on Locust while Stan worked behind us. I didn't trust him enough to leave his side so I could help Stan. I lost all track of time — it could have been minutes or hours I stood there while Stan recovered three VCRs, two TVs, and a stereo. He brought the items over one by one and laid them at my feet.

When he brought the last one over, he kept it in his arms. "That's everything. I mean, it's not everything I *lost*, but it's all that's here."

I eyed the small pile. "Okay. That's all we need." I bent down and stacked the VCRs on top of each other, topping it with one of the TVs, all the while keeping my gaze on Locust. Stan managed to get the rest of the merchandise in his arms and together, we sidestepped out of the apartment.

Locust mumbled something as he slammed the door in our faces. We didn't even look at each other as we bolted to the concrete steps, moving down them as quickly as we could without dropping the piles of electronics in our arms. When we made it to the bottom, we almost sprinted back to my truck, placing the items in the back seat as gently as we could manage in our rush. I couldn't stop myself from looking back over and over again. I just knew Locust would come running out, toting a gun in hand. I leapt into the driver's seat and started it up, throwing it in drive before Stan even pulled the passenger door shut.

We sped away from the apartment complex in broad daylight, meeting cars with ordinary people heading to work for the day. Funny – until recently, I was like them, living my life in oblivion to the other world that came alive when the sun went down. I knew about that world as a kid, riding in the back of the police car with my dad, but I never dreamed it would feel so close to home. When would Jeff wake up? When would he realize he didn't belong in that world? When would I have my little brother back? When would his daughters have their daddy back?

His girls entered my mind frequently, though I'm ashamed to admit I often pushed them out. They were teenagers now. They knew what was going on. They lived with Abigail, but Jeff still saw them frequently. Did they realize how severe the problem had become? Surely not. Surely Jeff put it all aside during his time with his girls. He wouldn't let anything get in the way of his relationship with them. Would he?

The truth was, I didn't know. I knew how much he loved those girls. I saw the way his eyes lit up when he talked about them, saw the way he doted on them while they played growing up and the patience he showed each of them as he taught them how to do things. The pride on his face when Christina caught her first fish brought tears to my eyes. They were his world back then. They still were. Weren't they?

I didn't allow myself to worry about the girls. I knew Abigail was taking care of them – they weren't in danger. They had food, clothing. They were going to school. So I didn't let myself think about what Jeff's addiction might be doing to them. It sounds selfish, I know, but I was so overwhelmed, so consumed by what it was doing to *me,* that when I thought about his girls hurting as well, it was just too much for me to handle. My plate was already overflowing; I was afraid if I added anything else to it, my mind would just shut down. It was hard enough to keep moving forward, to be the husband my wife needed and the dad my kids needed, while worrying constantly about Jeff.

I dropped Stan back at his store and helped him carry the items inside. In the bathroom, I changed out of my dark jeans and sweatshirt into my work clothes, and headed out to start my day. I was exhausted, yet filled with a strange adrenaline from the night's mission. We had done it. We had gotten back Stan's merchandise – not all of it, but a good chunk – and we came out unharmed. Maybe I'd failed over and over again when it came to my little brother, but I'd finally succeeded at one thing. If I couldn't clean him up, I could at least clean up one of the messes he left behind.

❊ ❊ ❊ ❊

Our success the night before gave us the confidence we needed to continue our mission. When I got off work, I went straight to the Rent-to-Own store. I yawned several times on the short drive. I knew when I got home and settled in my recliner, I'd be out like a light. But I didn't let my exhaustion ruin my momentum. It was time to confront Donald.

Since we had a number for Donald, we decided to try calling him first.

"Do you think he'll actually answer?"

I shrugged. "It's worth a shot, right?"

I dialed the number, doubting, like Stan, that he'd pick up the phone. But after the second ring, a deep voice greeted me. "Hello?"

"Hi, Donald?"

He paused. "Who's this?"

"My name's Jack. I understand you've been in business with my brother, Jeff Nolen."

Silence filled the line. "I don't know what you're talking about. I don't know anyone by that name."

I swallowed. Again, any nerves I felt were replaced by anger. I don't know why I was surprised by his denial, but I was. Did he think I was stupid? "I don't have much time, Donald, so don't waste it by lying to me. I'm calling you because I know for a fact you've been supplying my brother with crack cocaine. I also know he gave you some family antiques as trade. So let me tell you how this is going to work, okay?"

Beside me, Stan raised his eyebrows. Donald remained silent on the other end, so I continued. "I need that stuff back, Donald. All of it. And I have proof it's there. So the way I see it, I can get it back in one of two ways: one, you can give it to me yourself, or

64

two, I can send the cops over there to get it for me. So what will it be?"

Stan covered his mouth to stifle a laugh, though we both knew the situation really wasn't funny. It must have been so strange for him, seeing this other side of me – someone who made demands of a drug dealer with total confidence. But I knew that years of watching my dad on the job had prepared me for that moment. Somehow, I knew just what to say and how to say it.

Donald still hadn't spoken since I'd begun my speech. "What will it be, Donald?" I repeated.

Finally, he sighed. "I'll have it out on the porch in thirty minutes."

"We'll be there."

It wasn't until we pulled up outside the little gray house with the cluttered front porch that I remembered to be scared. I squinted at the edge of the driveway, feeling both relief and disgust when I spotted some of my grandmother's things among the mess. Heirlooms passed down through generations, sitting on the dirty porch of a dirty drug dealer. Would it really be that simple? Would Stan and I approach the porch, take my stuff in broad daylight, and drive away unharmed? No sign of life stirred around the house. Was someone waiting on the other side of the front door?

It was time to find out. I tucked my gun into my waistband again. Stan and I jumped out of the truck and took long, fast strides toward the porch. I climbed the rickety steps and immediately began pointing out her things. "Grab that. Can you carry this, too?" I grabbed as many items as I could carry, keeping my eyes on the door. When both of our arms were full, we took the load to the truck and went back to get the rest. Again, we filled our arms and carried the objects to the truck in silence, listening for any sign of someone approaching. This time, I was sure we had it all.

When I dropped Stan at his house that evening, the events of the past forty-eight hours suddenly weighed on my whole body. My shoulders ached with tension I hadn't realized I was carrying. My eyes were heavy, but I wasn't sure my mind would shut down long enough to let me sleep.

Lori stood in the doorway when I walked in. "Well? Did you get it all?"

I shook my head. "Not all. Most, though."

She looked me over. "You look exhausted." Then she pulled me to her, wrapping her arms around my waist and holding me tightly. Her voice shook as she added, "But at least you're in one piece."

I offered a weak smile, too tired to say anything else as I hugged her back. But her words echoed in my mind. *One piece.* Was I still in one piece? I didn't know anymore. It seemed the drugs that had stolen my brother had taken a piece of me, too.

Chapter Ten
Feeding the Addiction

During Jeff's short stay in rehab, we went into my grand-mother's house to clean up the place and move Jeff's things out. I didn't like the idea of letting him come out of rehab to find himself homeless, but we knew he couldn't stay there anymore. Not after the way he'd disrespected her stuff – disrespected *her*. He'd been allowed to live there for free, and he'd taken advantage of it. He had to make it on his own.

Inside the house, I found the deep freeze stocked full of concession items – assorted boxes of candy, gum, and other various items you might find at a ball game. Where had he found all that? He didn't seem to have a conscience when it came to stealing from others – he never did, even as a teen. But boxes of candy? Where had he even come across the opportunity to lift those items? What would he do with it all? Was there no limit to what he would take if the opportunity arose?

Once Stan and I recovered my grandmother's things, I hid the items in my house and hoped Jeff wouldn't find out what Stan and I had done – not because I cared what he might say about it, but because I didn't want him to try to steal the items for drug trade again. I looked around the house for the perfect hiding spot. *When Jeff comes over, what room is he least likely to go in?* I settled on a little closet in the hallway. As I placed the items on the shelves inside, my stomach knotted. Hadn't it been just a short time ago that the two of us were in and out of each other's houses all the time? Enjoying our families together? When did we reach the point that I had to hide things before he came over, fearing – knowing – that he would steal from me without a second thought?

Stan and I had the names of a couple other dealers we knew

supplied Jeff with drugs. We had no proof either one had any of the still-missing items, but feeling confident after our initial success with our missions, we decided it wouldn't hurt to at least check them out. Less than a week later, as I pulled away from the office after a long day of work, I went to pick up Stan for an evening drive around town.

It was already dark outside at five o'clock when I drove to Stan's house. We went straight to the project housing and cruised down the street, our eyes locked on the apartment at the end – a place police had been watching as well, I knew. We slowed to a crawl as we drove in front of it, then turned right to head toward the other side of town.

When I saw a black SUV with tinted windows and temporary plates pull out onto the street after me from across the road, I didn't think much of it. I drove up a couple blocks and then made a left, and the SUV followed me. I still didn't give it much thought, but for whatever reason, I absently looked in my rearview mirror to study the driver. The man I saw in my rearview mirror, with his hood pulled up and his seat leaned back, made my heart leap into my throat. He wasn't right on my tail, but I still got a strange feeling in my gut. Were we being followed?

I didn't say anything to Stan. I tried to laugh it off. *You're being paranoid. So what if this guy pulled out right behind you, made a couple of the same turns you made?*

But just in case, I made a quick left turn down a street I don't normally take.

The driver made the same turn.

I drove up a couple blocks, made a right and circled the block to put myself back out onto the street I'd just turned off of, this time going the opposite way, back toward the housing project. When I looked in my rearview mirror, the SUV was still behind us.

I took my sweaty palms off the steering wheel and wiped them on my pants. This was before the days that everyone had a cell phone, when I could have just called the police and had an officer escort me to scare him off. *What should I do? I can't lead this guy to either of our houses. Should I drive to the grocery store or some other public place? The police station?*

"Stan, I think we've got a little company."

Stan's narrowed eyes were already locked on the passenger-side mirror. "Yeah, I noticed."

While I tried to decide what to do, I made a little detour around town. I took more unexpected turns. When I cut across a dark alley and he continued to follow me, any doubt we were being followed was erased. My heart pounded out of my chest.

"Let's drive out of town. Toward Carrier Mills."

"Okay," I agreed. I could tell by the catch in Stan's voice he was as nervous as I was. I turned onto a rural road and headed out of town like Stan suggested.

The SUV started after us, but eventually turned and headed back toward Harrisburg. To be sure we lost him, I made a few more laps out on the country roads before taking a detour to Stan's house using as many back roads as I could manage. I dropped him off a couple blocks from his house just to be extra cautious. I then took an alternate route to my house, constantly looking over my shoulder. I hugged Lori and the kids a little tighter when I got home that evening and thanked God for watching over Stan and me.

I didn't see the SUV again, but I continued to keep a gun in my glove box when I left the house. I couldn't help but check my rearview mirrors every few minutes when I drove anywhere.

❖ ❖ ❖ ❖

Meanwhile, Jeff recovered from his wreck and found work doing contract labor at local coal mines. He had the certification and experience and as always, I found myself hopeful in the beginning. He was working again – that had to be a positive step, right? But when he lost more than one job over the course of the next year for being under the influence while working, I knew nothing had changed. If anything, things were getting worse.

He got back together with the young girl he dated before he ever left for rehab. He sold his house in town and cashed in the rest of his 401K from Sahara. In a nine-month period, he spent somewhere between eighty and one hundred and twenty thousand dollars. Much of it was wasted on drugs with nothing to show for the money. Some of it was spent on a new vehicle after he wrecked his own while under the influence. He didn't even really try to hide it from me anymore – he even admitted at one point that he was, once again, spending around a hundred dollars per day on crack cocaine for him and his girlfriend.

Life became a whirlwind for all of us as Jeff constantly ran into trouble with the law. In 1998, he was charged twice with disorderly conduct. His girlfriend got an order of protection against him in 1999. In early 2000, he dated and quickly married another girl, one who was known for "following drugs." Jeff fed her habit along with his own. In June of the same year, he went to jail after a police officer stopped him while he drove under the influence. He was charged with DUI, possession of meth, destroying evidence, obstructing justice, and possession of drug paraphernalia. The officers who booked him didn't search him well before taking him to jail – the fact that they had worked with and respected my dad made the situation a slightly awkward one. But since he had a knife on him that was later found, he was also charged with bringing a weapon into a penal institution.

He spent a few weeks in jail, held on a fifteen-hundred-dollar bond. It never even really crossed my mind to get him out – for one thing, I knew he needed to face the consequences for his actions, but it was also for my own peace of mind as well. I found that with Jeff in jail, I slept a little better at night. At least I didn't have to worry about where he was or what he was doing; I knew he was safe behind bars. It was bewildering. I never dreamed I'd see the day that my brother being in jail actually eased my stress and brought some comfort.

His wife eventually got him out, but Dad arranged to have one condition of his release include a weekly drug test. The two of them moved into a rental trailer just south of town, and Andrea, his middle daughter, moved in with them.

Andrea was fourteen years old when she moved back in with her dad. I had to admit, I was pleasantly surprised with her decision. All I could see was how good that might be for Jeff. Having someone in the house who depended on him would surely affect his decisions, right? Having someone he loved in his home all the time, someone he had to provide for, someone who needed him to keep his life together – that had to be a positive thing for him. Didn't it? Would his daughter's daily presence be the one thing he needed? The one thing that would bring my little brother back?

I hoped so. Through it all, I hadn't lost hope.

Andrea's sisters, Christina and Megan, both lived with Abigail. Christina and Andrea were Abigail's stepdaughters, but they had no contact with their real mother, and Abigail had always loved them like they were her own. I found out later that Andrea, who stayed close to her dad despite all his problems, realized the state he was in and moved back in with him to try to help him out. It wasn't easy for her to leave her sisters and the comfort of Abigail's home, but her dad needed her.

I was so relieved to see Andrea at home with her daddy that it took me much longer than it should have to realize he wasn't stepping up to be the father she needed. He loved her. Sometimes, when he looked at her, I saw a glimpse of the man he used to be, the man I knew he *could* be. But the drugs had a hold on him, preventing him from loving anyone more than he loved getting high. He couldn't give up his habits, and Andrea suffered for it.

It physically pains me to admit that I failed for months to see that Andrea was going to school without food in her stomach, without money for lunch. It never occurred to me he might not be providing for her until he called me one morning.

"Jack, I've run into a little trouble. I need you to help me out." My heart sank. *What now?* "What do you need, buddy?"

"I need money." When I didn't respond, he added, "For groceries. I just need to go to the store, get some food for the house. We...we're getting low. And I don't have any cash to get anything right now."

I sighed. "Let me talk to Lori. We'll see what we can do, okay?"

"Thank you. I promise...I won't let it happen again."

Lori and I knew better than to give Jeff cash for food. But we knew for Andrea's sake, we couldn't ignore his request, either. We had to take matters into our own hands.

That evening, when Jeff and his wife were gone and Andrea was alone in the trailer, Lori and I stopped by to visit her with bags of groceries. "Hey, sweetheart," I called when we walked inside. "We went shopping and ended up with some extra goodies. Could you guys use anything?"

Andrea practically leapt off the couch. "Food? What'd you bring?"

I set the bags down on the counter. "Take a look."

Andrea rummaged through the bags. She pulled out a package of lunch meat and opened it right away, pulling out pieces of turkey and shoving them in her mouth. Lori and I exchanged worried glances when she grabbed a bag of chips, ripped it open, and pulled out a giant handful. Clearly, she was hungry. She looked thin. Had she always been that thin?

Lori made her a sandwich and filled the rest of the plate with more chips and grapes. I opened the refrigerator to put the food inside, and my jaw dropped. It was empty. A case of beer, a half-empty bottle of ketchup, and some juice. No food. I glanced inside the cabinets. Bare as well. My stomach lurched.

"Andrea..." A lump formed in my throat. I swallowed it. "Is there...are you...is it always like this?" I gestured toward the cabinets. "No food?"

She shrugged. "Um...sort of. We...we haven't had much to eat around here lately."

I sighed. "Why didn't you say anything to us?"

She shrugged again and pasted on a smile. "I don't know. I just...I didn't want to worry you guys. It's no big deal, really."

Lori reached out and took her hand. "It is a big deal, honey. Will you promise me something? Next time, call me when you need something, okay? It can be between you and me. No one has to know about it, not even your dad. Okay?"

Andrea offered an embarrassed smile before she pulled Lori into a hug. "Thank you." Before we left, we slipped her some cash so she would have money to eat lunch at school.

I held my tears until after we left. It was the first time I stopped worrying about Jeff long enough to actually think about how his poor decisions were affecting everyone around him, including my nieces. What was going through the girls' heads, watching their father go to rehab, to jail? How were they coping with it all? Andrea was old enough to see the truth: her father was more worried about feeding his addictions than he was about feeding her. What would that do to her?

72

Chapter Eleven
The Stonefort Bank

Jeff had developed a reputation around town. He became the "usual suspect" when anything went wrong in Harrisburg. It almost became a sort of joke, in a sick way. Someone's car got broken into? Well, where was Jeff last night around that time? The thing about Jeff was, despite his addictions and his faults, he still had a way with people. He had a charm about him, something he'd had since he was just a little kid, that could make you forget for a few minutes what he was really capable of. I knew better than to leave him alone in my house…but it didn't stop me from inviting him over. I was used to his wild schemes, his half-baked plots he never followed through on. He was always half-jokingly suggesting some off-the-wall way to get rich quick, and most of the time, I didn't take him seriously.

Back at deer camp, a couple years before his addictions got the best of him, a group of us sat around a campfire in the evening. I don't remember what led to Jeff's comment, but I'll never forget what he said: "You know, if I was ever going to rob a bank, it'd be the one in Stonefort."

I smirked. "Oh, yeah?"

"Think about it. No cops nearby. Right there on the edge of town. It'd be a piece of cake. You could be in and out of there and halfway to Mexico before anyone knew what'd happened."

Chuckling, I shook my head. He had a point. "Yeah, I guess if someone was going to rob a bank, that'd be the way to go."

The conversation ended there, and I never gave it a second thought.

That is, until August 16, 2000, when I got a phone call that shook me to my core.

At nine-thirty in the morning, as I sat in my office in Marion, Illinois, my phone rang. My caller ID told me it was Stan. I leaned back in my chair. "Hey, buddy. How's it going?"

"Did you hear the news?"

I raised my eyebrows. "What news?"

"Someone robbed the Stonefort Bank."

"Really?"

We both just sat there for a moment, lost in our own thoughts. We didn't say a word – we didn't *have* to say a word. We were both thinking the same thing: *he did it*. I knew in my gut he did it. And not just because of the comment he made at deer camp years before. I just *knew*. I can't explain it; something inside of me knew it had to be true.

Over the course of the day, more details came out regarding the robbery. Someone had gone inside with a mask, possibly with a gun, and demanded the money in the drawers.

The FBI got involved. Like always, Jeff became a suspect. In the days following the incident, Jeff spent over a thousand dollars on various elaborate, unnecessary purchases. My chest ached. Where had he gotten that money? How was he able to afford a new flat-screen TV when not long ago, he couldn't even afford groceries?

But he had an explanation for that. He and his wife had gone to the boat in Metropolis the weekend before the robbery, where Jeff had a very lucky night of gambling. He won an eighteen hundred dollar jackpot, as well as a couple other smaller ones for a few hundred dollars each. They spent the night down there in the casino hotel. A State Police investigator who had worked with my dad and was still a close friend of the family checked out the story and as it turned out, it was true. "I honestly don't think he did it," he told Dad and me one evening.

I wasn't so sure. I wanted to believe it, of course. This investigator had questioned Jeff. He knew him – knew his history and what he was capable of doing. He knew better than to be naïve when it came to Jeff and his incredible ability to lie. If he believed my brother was innocent, wasn't there a chance he actually was?

Though Jeff's story turned out to be true, he failed his weekly drug test. A warrant went out for his arrest, and Jeff went back to jail.

Andrea still stayed at his house from time to time, but by that point, she was eighteen and wasn't home often. About a week after Jeff was locked up, his wife moved in with another man — one also known for drugs. So, no one stayed in the trailer Jeff had.

At nine thirty one night, almost two weeks since he'd been in jail, he called Stan. "I need you to go to my house and do something for me."

"What's that?"

"You have to go in my house and get something out of there for me."

"Okay...what is it?"

"Some cash. It's hidden in a plastic grocery bag in the air vent in Andrea's bedroom."

"Aw, Jeff, I don't know if I should —"

"You have to! Please. I promise, it's nothing illegal or anything like that. It's where I hide any cash I've saved. I'm afraid my wife will come back there and tear the place apart looking for the money while I'm away. If she finds it, she...she'll blow through it all. Please, Stan. I can't lose that money."

Stan hesitated. As far as we knew, his wife wasn't coming around the trailer. We knew she wanted to avoid the law and figured she'd keep her distance from the place. And besides, did he really want to get in the middle of this? Did he want to move what was possibly stolen money and put himself at risk for trouble?

But Stan ultimately decided to give Jeff the benefit of the doubt. After all, if the investigator from the Illinois State Police believed he was innocent in all this, who was he to doubt? Maybe this money was the cash he had won at the boat that night.

He called me as soon as he hung up the phone with Jeff. Like Stan, I had my reservations. Was this a good idea? Were we getting ourselves involved in something we shouldn't? But I wanted to believe my brother, and like always, I wanted to help him. I wanted so badly to think he was innocent, though his name wasn't completely cleared yet in the investigation. And the more

▲Me and Jeff - 1965

▲Me and Jeff before my cousin's wedding - 1973

▲Mom, Dad, me and Jeff - 1975

Me and Jeff at Christmas - 1974

▲Dad - 1990, shortly before he retired from the State Police

◄Jeff's 14th Birthday

▲Jeff - 1990, 27 years old

▲Jeff - 1992

▲Jeffrey working underground - 1992

Jeff and Stan - Oct. 20, 1994 ▶

▲Jeff - 1994

Deer Season 1994 ▶
Front: Me, Stan,
Lori's cousin Troy
kneeling in back: My
brother-in-law Terry
standing in back: Jeff

▲Stan and Jeff

Stanley, Elizabeth, Zachery and
Alexa Hutchison - May 2002

▲Me and Lori

◀Front: Lori with Gavin on her lap, Brooklyn, Gunner. Back: Jackson, Me and Tiffany.

▲Jackson's graduation from Police Academ - Dec. 2013 Front (L-R) Gavin and Gunne Back: Tiffany, Carol, Me, Jackson, Jackson wife Taylor, and Lori.

▲ Lori and Me with Brooklyn, Gunner and Gavin.

▶Jeff's mugshot - December 2013

I considered it, the more I convinced myself the money must have come from his gambling winnings. I knew he was right – if his wife did happen to search the place and find it, she'd spend it all on drugs while he was gone. So, I did what I thought I had to do. I had to help my little brother.

After the kids had gone to bed, I left the house to pick up Stan and the two of us drove to Jeff's. It was pitch black inside and outside of the trailer. We parked behind it and broke in through a window in the back. We climbed inside with nothing but flashlights, going straight to Andrea's room without a word. When we pulled the cover off the air vent, sure enough, there lay the plastic bag. Stan tucked it under his shirt and we climbed back out and jogged to my truck.

When I was back out on the road, Stan dared to open the bag. I watched out of the corner of my eye while he counted the money inside. "Seventeen hundred dollars," he announced.

I sighed in relief. "Well, that's gotta be the money from the boat, right? He won eighteen hundred bucks that night, plus a few hundred more; that has to be what's left of it."

Stan nodded. "Makes sense."

I felt better about what we'd just done, but I wasn't sure what to do with the money, so I drove to Dad's. We filled him in on the night's events while he listened with furrowed eyebrows.

"We just weren't sure where to take it, Dad. Any suggestions?"

Dad frowned. "Well, to be honest, I don't want it here. You're probably right – it probably is the money he won. But while all this is going on, I just...I mean, until we know for sure, I don't..."

"We can put it in my office," Stan offered. By this point, Stan had sold his Rent-to-Own business and owned a tax preparation company.

So, when Stan and I left Dad's house, we drove to Stan's office and put the money up in one of the ceiling tiles. We didn't talk much as we drove home, and I knew he was thinking about what we'd just done, like I was. I convinced myself the money wasn't stolen, even though the little pit in my stomach put a seed of doubt in my mind. After all, this was Jeff we were dealing with. I could never be sure of anything. But I knew my brother – the

Chapter Eleven - The Stonefort Bank

real one, the one I'd grown up with – was still inside there somewhere. And I just knew he was going to come back to me someday. He'd already been through so much, already been through rehab and time in jail…wasn't he close to that "rock bottom" I'd heard about? Wouldn't he get it together soon? Maybe this time, when he came out of jail, he really would be tired of living his life this way. Maybe this would be the last straw, the thing that would wake him up and make him realize he was better than this. He was meant for so much more than this.

I couldn't give up on him. And I knew God wouldn't, either. He didn't put my brother here in this world so he'd waste his life with this addiction. I threw up a prayer, the same one I offered day after day after day: *God, open Jeff's eyes. Let him see what he's doing to himself and to those around him who love him. Please, just bring my brother back to me.*

The next day, the local optometrist called Mom to let her know Jeff's glasses, which had broken just a couple days before he went to jail, were fixed. Mom offered to go get them for Jeff, so he called Stan and asked him to get sixty dollars out of the bag in the ceiling of his office and give it to Mom.

As big as this world is, God still has a way of making things come together and intertwine in such incredible ways. As it turned out, the wife of the investigator with the Illinois State Police – the one who believed Jeff was innocent – worked at the optometrist's office. Mom went into the office and paid for Jeff's glasses with the money Stan had given her. When the investigator's wife told her husband what had happened, he took the sixty dollars my mom had used to pay.

As it turned out, the serial numbers on those bills matched the money that had been stolen from the Stonefort Bank.

The FBI was involved almost immediately. The next morning, I got a call at work, letting me know that an FBI agent and an Illinois State Police investigator from the Department of Criminal Investigation were on their way to my office.

At the same time, another FBI agent and a different ISP investigator went to Stan's office as well.

My heart raced. I knew I was innocent; I wasn't worried about me or Stan getting in trouble for our role in it all. I would tell them the truth and help however I could. But a weight settled in on my shoulders as I waited for them to arrive at my office. *He did it. My brother. He actually did it. He robbed a bank.* All those thoughts I'd had about him being close to rock bottom...I had no idea he had so much farther to fall. He'd been in trouble before, but this made all those previous incidents look like child's play, like that rowdy boy he used to be, looking to find a little mischief in the neighborhood. What would happen to him now? What would this do to our family?

I groaned as that thought brought another thought to mind. Dad. Our poor dad. He dedicated his whole life to upholding the law. Everything he stood for, everything he fought against, broken by his own son. When I thought about all the things that must be going through his mind, my heart ached for him. I knew that, like me, he blamed himself for Jeff's problems. He never really said it, but he didn't have to. I knew he questioned himself constantly. *What could I have done differently? What could I have said to him that might have changed the path he took?*

I watched out my office window as the unmarked black police car pulled into the parking lot and prayed that their presence wouldn't cause a scene. Jeff had brought on more than enough embarrassment for me at my place of employment over the years. Luckily, it happened to be a day that most everyone was out of the office, including my boss, who worked out of Virginia at the time. Two men worked in their offices nearby, but I didn't tell them what was going on, though I figured they'd hear about it on the evening news anyway. I met the FBI agent and the investigator at the door and shook their hands. I somewhat knew the DCI investigator from back when Dad used to work for that department. I introduced myself to them both before showing them to my office and closing the door behind us.

As I sat down across from the two men and wiped my sweaty palms on my pants, I remembered something my dad told me years before: *always tell the truth, and you won't have to wonder about what you said.* I had nothing to hide. Remembering that calmed me a little.

Both men were professional. They were courteous, but very matter-of-fact as they drilled me with questions over the next two hours. It became intense at times, but I expected nothing less. They were just doing their jobs. After all, Stan and I had stolen bank money in our possession and their job was to find out why. I knew they would compare the stories we gave them in order to get to the bottom of who was and who wasn't involved. I didn't hold anything back as I recalled the night Jeff asked Stan to move the money from his house. I explained that I gave my brother the benefit of the doubt as to where that money had come from, though as it turned out, I shouldn't have. Once again, he'd lied to me. To all of us. And as I had so many times before, I let myself believe him anyway.

The facts from that day came out slowly. Incredibly, my brother and his wife had the nerve to use Mom's car, which held a license plate that said, "Nolen10," as their getaway car. I'm sure my eyes almost popped out of my head when that piece was revealed. Were they really that ignorant? Or just that brazen? His wife drove the car and dropped him off. He entered the bank wearing camo bib overalls, a long-sleeved T-shirt, a hat, a bandana, and gloves. He kept one hand in his overalls and demanded money, not actually claiming to have a gun but leading the teller to believe he did. The teller gave him all the money in the drawer – probably much to Jeff's surprise. Once he had the money, he jumped back in the car and changed clothes while his wife sped away. He put the clothes he'd worn in a bag that he weighed down and threw in an old strip pit before the two drove back into town as if nothing had ever happened.

Though the story Stan gave the two men at his office matched my own, the investigators still weren't through. That evening, they came to my house for an additional two hours of questioning. Lori and Mom sat at the table with Stan and me, along with two investigators – one FBI and one DCI – and listened as Stan and I fielded question after question.

I glanced over at Mom when I heard her sigh. I knew the look she wore on her face – Jeff and I had seen it ourselves many times in our lives. She was growing impatient. And the longer she sat there, the more irritated she became, until she finally couldn't hold back any longer. "Now, just a minute. That's about enough questions for tonight, don't you think? You've spent hours here today, looking for a story you're not going to find. They've already told you they don't know anything about it, and they're not going to come up with any new information for you. You should be ashamed of yourself, badgering innocent boys this way."

I reached across the table and grabbed her hand, hoping to calm her down. "Mom, this is their job. Let them do it."

But to my surprise, the FBI agent got a kick out of her rant. He chuckled, and soon he had her laughing as well.

I spent my fortieth birthday in Benton, Illinois, at the federal courthouse where Stan and I were called to testify, listening to a grand jury hand down the indictment for bank robbery. As it turned out, because the robbery was not actually *armed* robbery, his sentence would be four to five years. But Jeff was smart. His history of drugs was no secret, so he did what he knew he had to do in order to get that sentence reduced: he started talking. He cooperated with law enforcement, giving them information about some of the higher-up drug dealers in order to get his sentence reduced. When the trial ended, he was served with a two-and-a-half year sentence in a federal prison in Terra Haute, Indiana.

I walked out of that courthouse with a deep sadness in the pit of my stomach, knowing my little brother would be locked away and how difficult this would be for our family, especially Dad. Jeff was thirty-seven years old. What would he do from here, when it was all over? Would the time in prison be what he needed to finally reflect on the choices he had made to bring him to this point?

At the same time, I couldn't deny the strange sense of relief I felt. Once again, it would be a little break from worrying about him all the time – at least we'd know he was safe, he had food, and he wasn't able to get the drugs that had ruined his life. Maybe, in a weird way, this was an answer to the prayers I threw up to God in desperation every night. Maybe this would be his chance to really get clean and make some changes. Maybe he'd come out with a new attitude.

I think his absence hit me hardest at deer camp the first year he was away. As we sat around a campfire that first evening, my chest ached. My brother had been with us at camp every single year since we were kids – though I had to admit, the last few years while deep in his addiction, he wasn't really "there." Still, as I looked at that empty spot next to me where he always sat, I was overwhelmed by the fact that life as I knew it would never be the same again. Even when he was free, he would never come back to camp. A convicted felon couldn't have a gun.

My family struggled through two and a half years of holidays – family dinners with the same empty place at the table. Though we didn't talk about it much, trying not to upset each other, I knew his absence weighed on all of our minds. It was like a piece of me was gone, too, like a hole torn in my heart only my little brother could fill. That hole wasn't new; it'd been there for years, as I'd lost my brother years before he actually went away. But I couldn't describe how much I missed him. Even though I couldn't trust him, even though I worried about him with every passing second, I wished he was sitting at the table with the rest of us. I longed to hear his infectious laughter and his wild, entertaining stories.

For those two and a half years, I threw myself into my family and my job, quietly counting down the months until my brother would be free again. Soon, those remaining months became few enough that I could count down the days. Every time I thought about his release, my heart leapt into my throat. I wanted to see him. I wanted to pick him up outside the prison. Over and over, I imagined the reunion we would have. Jeff would laugh, maybe even shed a few tears, and tell me how the time away from his daughters had changed his life. He would come back home to start over. A new life. One that didn't include drugs.

I didn't allow myself to entertain the little shadow of doubt fluttering in my stomach every time that fantasy played in my mind. Because if this wasn't rock bottom, what was? Things could only get better from here.

This was it. This was what he needed to get his life back on track. It *had* to be. For him. For his daughters. For all of us.

My Brother's Keeper

Chapter Twelve
The Release of the Caged Animal

I'll never forget the day Stan and I were finally reunited with Jeff after those long, painful two and a half years. As we stood there inside that prison, waiting to pick him up and bring him home, I couldn't wipe the smile from my face. Any worry, any doubt, was pushed to the back of my mind. My only thought was on seeing my brother.

When he finally stood in front of me and pulled me into a hug, something inside of me released. I couldn't hold back the tears as I hugged him back. "It's so good to see you."

"It's good to see you, too, brother."

I watched as he hugged Stan, my heart soaring. He was free. He was coming home.

But I'll never forget the look in his eyes when he pulled away. The only way to describe it was *wild*. Like an animal who had been caged for too long.

Jeff left prison that day with a prescription in hand and asked us to stop at a pharmacy to fill it for him. On the drive home, I learned that he had been kept on a sedative during his time in prison.

My chest deflated as I watched him and listened to him talk. Where was that changed man I just knew would be sitting in my truck? Had the last two and a half years been for nothing? Hadn't he reflected on his life and saw the way drugs had taken everything that mattered?

As soon as he got home, he started making up for lost time. The first thing he did was steal Mom's credit card and head to Sears, where he bought tools and an air conditioner – items he could trade for drugs. He racked up a bill for thousands of dollars, all in her name.

Mom was devastated. She showed me the bill, and I immediately knew what had happened, though it didn't make it any less shocking. I stared at the bill. "Mom," I said when I found my voice, "you have to do something."

"I can't afford that. What am I going to do?"

I shook my head. "You're not paying the first cent. You...you have to turn him in."

Mom's mouth opened and then closed again. She sighed. "Jack, I can't do that."

"Mom, you have to. What choice do you have? He...*stole* from you. You have to report it."

She bit her lip as tears formed in her eyes. "He's still my son. I...I just can't..."

My chest ached for her. I took a step forward and put my hands on her shoulders, looking into her eyes. "Mom, you can't...protect him from this. You said yourself you can't afford it." I took a deep breath and dropped my hands. "I know it won't be easy. Trust me, I don't want to see him in trouble again any more than you do. But...Jeff needs help," I sighed and said aloud the realization that was finally setting in. "He needs help we can't give him. And if we allow him to get away with this kind of stuff, we...we're only contributing to the problem."

The tears spilled over onto her cheeks. She stared at me, seeming to consider my words. Finally, she nodded.

Mom's hands shook as she dialed the number for the local police. Tears continued to stream down her face as she reported her card stolen and admitted she knew who had taken it. When she hung up, I could literally see the change that seemed to take place inside of her. She had done something she never thought she'd have to or would even be capable of doing – she had turned in her baby boy.

My grandmother – Dad's mother – passed away just two days after Jeff was released from prison. As we planned her funeral, my daughter developed a terrible ear infection and was prescribed medication to help her deal with the pain. Grief and stress overwhelmed our whole family. It was a small distraction from my constant worries about Jeff.

During the visitation, I noticed Dad sitting alone with tears in his eyes. I put on what I hoped was a brave face before I walked over, leaned down and hugged him. "You okay, buddy?"

He hugged me back without answering. When he pulled away, he sighed and looked me straight in the eyes. "Always remember this, Jack: Life's tough, and it's not always fair. But the sun will still come up tomorrow. You have to get up and keep marching, even when you don't feel like it. Because someone is always counting on you."

I nodded, letting his words soak in, and thought about all the people who were counting on me. My wife, my kids. My boss. And most importantly, God. I knew I hadn't been fully there for any of them the last few years, God included. I'd been there physically, but mentally I was often miles away, my mind consumed with my brother.

When his face entered my mind, I scanned the crowd behind us and found him. I knew immediately he was on something – he could barely hold his head up in the back of the room.

Anger burned inside my chest. Here he was, drugged out of his mind, at our grandma's funeral. How could he do this? How could he be so careless? Did he have no respect for our family, for our Dad? Did he truly care about no one but himself?

After the funeral, Andrea found an empty pill bottle in the trash can at Mom's. When she handed it to me, my heart sank. It was my daughter's medication, the pain pills she'd received just a day and a half earlier. A full bottle, designed to last weeks, gone in less than two days.

I stared at that bottle, then looked up at Andrea and shook my head. "Unbelievable."

Her nostrils flared. She snatched the bottle from my hands. "I'm calling him out on it."

My jaw dropped. "Oh, honey, I don't know if you should – "

But before I could finish my sentence, she spun on her heels and walked away from me. I followed her into the living room, my head spinning. "Andrea, why don't you wait? There are a lot of people here, and your dad...he might get – "

She didn't even seem to hear me. When she reached Jeff, she thrust the empty bottle in his face. "What's this, Dad?"

He eyed the bottle, finally coherent enough to hold his head fairly steady. "Looks like Tiffany's medicine."

"Yeah. Tiffany's medicine, which she just got *yesterday morning* for her ear infection. And it's empty today. Empty!"

Jeff's eyes narrowed. "I don't know what you're trying to say."

"You know exactly what I'm trying to say, Dad." Andrea's voice lost its edge. She swallowed. "You took them. You stole from...from your own niece. And you made a scene at Grandma's funeral because you were all...messed up."

When Jeff leapt off the couch, I stepped forward. I didn't really think he'd harm his own daughter, but I didn't trust the look on his face. Fire blazed in his eyes. "How dare you. How dare you accuse me of something like that."

Andrea didn't seem fazed by his anger. She threw her hands up in the air. "Are you really going to stand here and try to tell me you didn't take these pills?"

He stared at her, and I took another step forward until I could have reached out and touched him. I'd seen Jeff mad more than once and knew how quickly things could turn violent. He shook his head. "You have some nerve." His eyes traveled around the now-silent room, eyeing each of us. "Which one of you did it, huh? Who stole the pills and planted that bottle to frame me?"

I crossed my arms over my chest. "Jeff, come on. You don't really expect us to think you didn't steal those pills, do you?"

He ran his hands through his hair, grunting and snorting in anger. "This...this is ridiculous. I don't have to listen to this. I don't have to stay here and put up with it." He turned and headed toward the door.

I started after him. "Jeff, wait —"

He whipped around to face me and shoved a finger into my chest. *"Don't* follow me."

So I didn't. I stood frozen and watched him storm through the back door, slamming it behind him.

We didn't see him again for three days.

Tiffany and I were at Mom's house when he returned after those three days. My daughter played in the backyard while I sat in the living room with Mom, who was distraught beyond words by Jeff's disappearance. When I heard the car pull into the driveway, I watched out her picture window. It was my brother. His appearance both relieved me and broke my heart. He still wore the same clothes he'd had on when he left. His unkempt hair was greasy. I knew by his twitchy mannerisms he had been on a three-day drug bender and probably hadn't slept at all.

I steeled myself for the coming hostility. Between Grandma's funeral and the incident with the pain pills, I hadn't yet been able to confront him regarding Mom's stolen credit card.

When he walked inside, I took a deep breath. I didn't even let him take off his shoes and settle in before I approached him. "Jeff, we need to talk."

His red eyes flicked toward me. "Not now. I just got here."

"This can't wait."

He shook his head, muttering under his breath.

I ignored him. "We know you stole the credit card. Mom's got thousands of dollars of charges to deal with because of you."

Jeff's eyes grew wide. "Are you serious? I just walked in the door, and already you're accusing me of some...some nonsense?" My mouth opened, but at that moment, nothing came out. His ability to stand there and stare straight into my eyes and continue to lie even when he knew he'd been caught astounded me. The look on his face – so innocent, as if he was a victim – infuriated me.

I finally found my voice. "Don't waste my time by lying, Jeff. We know you did it, know you bought that stuff to trade for drugs."

In seconds, he closed the distance between us until his nose almost touched mine. Spit sprayed from his mouth as he screamed at me. "Get out of here, Jack! Get out of this house, and out of my life!"

My blood boiled in my veins and when I spoke, the volume of my voice matched his. "Oh, you want me out of your life? I'm one of the only people left who still cares enough to be here! You're stealing from your own family just to feed your habit and don't even care who you hurt in the process as long as you can stay high all the time! I don't –"

My words were cut short by his fist in my jaw. I jerked back, surprised for only a moment before I recovered and returned the blow. Vaguely, I heard Mom crying in the background, begging us to stop, but in seconds, the two of us were rolling around on the floor, wrestling just as we'd done that day I showed up and forced him to go to rehab. Only this time, the fight was more vicious. We were out for blood.

I was so engrossed in the fight, I didn't see or hear Tiffany come in the back door. But when she saw us, she ran home and told my wife what was happening in the middle of her grandmother's house. Lori called the police and within minutes, two officers showed up in Mom's driveway. Though I hadn't noticed my own daughter's presence, the two men in uniform approaching us finally got my attention. I yanked myself free from Jeff's grasp and scooted back, panting as I put distance between us and raised my hands in surrender.

Jeff's eyes were still wild. He continued to yell belligerently, resisting arrest until one officer doused his face with pepper spray. He screamed as they cuffed him and led him outside. Mom and I watched from the doorway as they put him in the back of the car and drove away.

Only nine days out of prison, Jeff was taken back to jail on parole violation and misuse of a credit card. This time, he was sentenced to a federal prison in Ashland, Kentucky. If his first prison sentence put a strain on our family, this one almost broke us all. I wrestled with devastation, guilt, and a strange feeling of relief that came with knowing at least when he was in prison, he was safe.

But above everything, my stomach still ached with the empty feeling that came from losing my brother yet again. He just continued to slip further and further away from me, and I was losing hope that my brother, my real brother, would ever come back to me. I continued on with my life – Lori, the kids, work – went about my daily routine with a fake smile on my face and pretended everything was okay. But inside, that piece of me was still missing. I tried to pray about it, but many days, I couldn't find any words to say. And so I said the same thing over and over again: *God, please...just bring my brother back to me.*

Chapter Thirteen
A Changed Man

I have to admit, when Stan and I drove to pick up Jeff the day he was released about a year and a half after he'd left, I still didn't harbor much hope. I'd been let down so many times before. That same hole persisted inside of me – the one that had throbbed and tortured me so badly during his first stint in prison – but somehow, its presence didn't feel quite the same. I was strangely numb.

On the drive to Ashland, Kentucky, I kept the conversation light and tried not to entertain any thoughts of finding this changed man in place of my brother. With each painful, disappointing moment, my heart built its own wall around it that hope struggled to penetrate.

But as soon as Jeff and I made eye contact for the first time, even my guarded heart couldn't stop the flutter in my stomach. It was my brother, and something was...different. There was a light in his eyes I hadn't seen in years. When he grabbed me and pulled me to him, hugging me tighter than he ever had before, my eyes grew wide. "Jack, it's so good to see you." He pulled away to look me in the eyes, then hugged me again. "I...I'm so sorry. For everything."

Tears streamed down my cheeks. With that one little apology, the wall around my heart crumbled. My little brother, my best friend – he was back. Could this be real? Did something happen? Did something sink in this time that had never sunk in before?

I couldn't help but glance over at him constantly on the drive home. I waited for him to pull a prescription from his pocket, waited for that wild look to return to his eyes. But with each easy smile he gave me, my shoulders relaxed a little more. He and Stan laughed, and it was like old times, like he'd never even left. I listened as he talked about getting back home to see his girls and even mentioned a place he planned to apply for a job, and the knot in my chest began to loosen. A little voice somewhere deep inside of me screamed out in protest. *Don't let your guard down just yet. Don't get your hopes up.* But I buried it. After all these years, my brother finally seemed like himself again. This was the answer to my prayers...wasn't it?

With each passing day, I became more convinced it was. Dad and my new stepmom, Carol, helped him get a little house in town. I reached out to some contacts to help him get a job as a contract miner in Western Kentucky. He reconnected with his daughters. When he laughed, his eyes glistened with that mischievous spark he'd had before, the one that had been clouded over by the constant stream of drugs inside of him.

One Saturday afternoon, I watched him as he sat on the couch in my living room, playing a video game with Jackson. The two of them bantered back and forth, Jeff teasingly mocking Jackson as he struggled to defeat a level, when I blurted out, "Hey, Jeff, why don't you come to church with us tomorrow morning?"

Jeff didn't take his gaze off the television, but he seemed to consider my question. I held my breath, waiting for him to come out with some excuse as to why he couldn't. But then, to my surprise, he looked over at me and nodded once. "Okay."

My heart leapt into my throat, and I blinked back tears. I sat in my recliner, trying to control the wide smile that threatened to spread across my face. *Okay, God. I'm going to get him there. Now You can work Your magic on him.*

Lori, Tiffany, Jackson, and I pulled into his driveway the next morning, and I half-expected to have to go inside and drag him out of bed. But before we'd even parked, he came out his front door wearing jeans and a button-down shirt. Lori sucked in a breath. "Well, look at him, all cleaned up."

I laughed. "He looks good."

"Better than he has in years," Lori agreed.

He hopped in the back of the car next to Jackson. "Hey, buddy." He jabbed an elbow in my son's side. Jackson grunted and returned the gesture.

I couldn't wipe the grin off my face as we backed out of the driveway and headed to church. The hole that had gaped open for so long was finally closing in. My brother was home. He was healthy. He was happy. For the first time in years, I felt complete. *Thank You, God. Thank You for doing what didn't seem possible. Thank You for putting this nightmare behind us. But please, keep working on him. Speak to him today.*

The preacher gave a sermon about putting all trust and hope in God, even when, through human eyes, things looked impossible. Again, I thanked God. *These last few years looked so bleak, but You still had control. Why is it so easy for me to forget that? Thank You for watching over my brother through it all.*

It was one of those sermons when I just knew the message was meant for me. I became so engrossed in it, I didn't realize my brother was sitting next to me, feeling that the sermon was meant for him, too. When the message ended and the soft piano music filled the sanctuary, the preacher stood in front of the room. "If you have anything in your life that is keeping you from God, please, leave it up here at the altar this morning. If you feel Him speaking to your heart, don't turn Him away. Step out into that aisle and come forward. Let us pray with you. Don't leave here today, still carrying that burden with you."

I prayed silently in the pew when I felt my brother shift next to me. My eyes fluttered open just in time to see him rise to his feet and step out into the aisle. My jaw dropped as I watched him move to the front of the room. When he reached the altar, he fell to his knees.

Tears welled as I stared at him. The preacher knelt down beside him, and the two of them whispered back and forth for a moment before the preacher covered Jeff's hand with his own and they both bowed their heads. I looked over at Lori, who stared at me with wide, sparkling eyes. When she jerked her head toward the front, I snapped out of my trance. *Go up there and pray with him,* I heard in my heart.

I jumped to my feet and almost jogged down that aisle. When I reached Jeff, I bent down behind him, resting my hand on his shoulder. The tears flowed over onto my cheeks. My mind spun, making it impossible to gather my thoughts enough to pray a coherent prayer. Instead, I repeated the same thing over and over again. *Thank You, God. Thank You. Thank You, God.*

Jeff made a decision to follow Jesus that morning. My chest felt so full I thought it would burst. I could have whooped and hollered and sprinted around the sanctuary, but instead, I just grabbed my brother and held him in a hug. Everything I'd ever wanted for my brother was unfolding right before my eyes.

Over the next month, Jeff grew closer to the preacher's daughter. She was divorced with a young daughter, and she and Jeff hit it off right away. I was elated, of course. Our whole family was thrilled. Maryanne was a good woman; Jeff needed one of those. When I saw him walk into church and sit down with her and her daughter, saw that adorable little girl look up at Jeff and giggle when he leaned down to tease her, I smiled until my cheeks ached.

I didn't miss the worried glances exchanged between the preacher and his wife, and I understood them. Why *wouldn't* they be worried about a match like this? This was their daughter, after all. She was newly-divorced. Vulnerable. There was the little girl to think about. Any man coming into the picture would make them nervous. And Jeff? A twice-convicted criminal, fresh out of jail? Any parent would be entitled to a panicky reaction, even a man who preaches love and forgiveness for a living.

But all I could see was how good *she* would be for *him.* He seemed to be on the right path in his life, and having a woman like Maryanne by his side would only help ensure he stayed on it. A few short months later, at the same altar where Jeff gave his life to Jesus, he pledged his heart to Maryanne. Her daughter stood up with them as they vowed to love each other forever.

All that weight that had pressed on my shoulders and chest for years finally lifted. Even my sleep patterns changed – I no longer woke up through the night in a cold sweat, wide-eyed, with no idea what had upset me. Everything was just as it should be. We'd been to hell and back and God had brought us through it. What could possibly go wrong now?

Chapter Fourteen
Back Into The Wilderness

If there's one thing I've learned about Satan, it's this: never underestimate him.

I know our God is stronger than the devil will ever be. Satan knows that, too. And I guess I used to think when he lost one of his to the light, he'd let it be. The Bible tells us the way things will go in the end, after all. Why would Satan keep fighting a battle God had already won? Why chase after someone who had chosen Jesus? There are plenty of other people out there – why waste his time on a new Christian?

How wrong I was. Satan won't bother much with those who don't know Jesus. He doesn't have to; he already has their heart. What does he need them for? It's those who find Jesus, those who finally get a glimpse of the truth and what their lives *could* be if Jesus runs the show, that he feels the need to fight for.

I wholeheartedly believe there's a reason why, in the Bible, after Jesus was baptized, the very next chapter tells us that He was led into the wilderness to be tempted by the devil. That's what Satan does; it's who he is. He waits until he's losing us, until we've seen a vision of life without him and choose that life, and then he strikes.

I know in my soul when Jeff gave his heart to Jesus that morning, he meant it. I saw the look on his face when he finished praying at that altar. But he was like one of those seeds Jesus talks about, one that fell on rocky ground and sprang up quickly. Like that plant that shot up, when the sun came up, Jeff was scorched. He received God's love with joy and excitement but didn't take the time to let his roots develop. There was no depth to sustain his growth. And because of this, he was vulnerable.

And Satan swooped in.

He and Maryanne were barely settled into their marriage

when some of Jeff's friends from his other life started coming around again. And I know he tried to do right and stay on this new path; I *know* he was fully aware of just how far he'd come and didn't want that addiction to consume him again. But for whatever reason, his head and his heart couldn't line up on what was best for him.

I will never understand what it is in an addict that draws them, sometimes drags them kicking and screaming to the one thing that is destroying them. Jeff was clean. He'd managed to break loose of those chains. He fought the dragon and did the unthinkable – he won. He escaped addiction and reclaimed the life Jesus wanted for him, the one he'd intended for him since the day he was conceived. But Satan crept back inside his mind, slowly and carefully, and whispered the same lies he'd told him back when we were kids. *Just doing it once in a while won't hurt anything. It doesn't make you a bad person. You're stronger than you used to be. You won't let it get the best of you this time. You work hard; you deserve a break. Just something to take the edge off.*

When it comes to addiction, it doesn't matter how hard you try – if you keep gravitating toward the same people, the same places, putting yourself in Satan's path, you *will* fail. And that's exactly what Jeff did.

It happened so fast, we didn't have time to stop and question how and when it even started again. One day, he was working steadily and living a fairytale with Maryanne and her little girl, and the next day, he wrecked another vehicle on his way home from work. The little sensor in my chest went off immediately. I knew what it meant all those other times he wrecked a truck. But he blamed it on a deer, and in our rural area, that's nothing out of the ordinary. I believed him and pushed that little worry as far back in my brain as I could. My mind wasn't ready to face it again; my emotions couldn't handle another round.

Like me, Maryanne chose to believe his story. But their happy life together began to shift in their home. He slowly morphed into a man she didn't recognize. His pleasant demeanor began to change. His full-of-life personality was clouded by a darkness she wasn't familiar with. He wasn't home, wasn't present in their lives in the same way he once was. She caught him in little white lies. These small things snowballed into something bigger, something Maryanne wasn't prepared to – and shouldn't have had to – deal with.

And so she packed up her daughter and her things, and she left him.

Before I could blink, things spiraled out of control all over again. Some pieces from a local jewelry store turned up missing, and Jeff's name was brought to the table as a suspect. When the police showed up at his house to question him, they found him passed out in his recliner with the jewelry lying on the table next to him. He was taken to jail but was somehow able to post his own bond and come home.

A week and a half later, Mom got a notice from her bank that she had overdrawn her account by eight hundred dollars. In that short time since he'd gotten out of jail, he managed to steal Mom's checkbook and blew through three thousand six hundred dollars before we ever even realized what had happened.

Mom was forced to press charges against him in order to avoid having to pay it all back herself. Her devastation was indescribable. She obsessed over it, dwelled on it, until it consumed her every thought. Soon after, she started having difficulties with memory loss, and all at once, Alzheimer's and dementia came on strong. Was this a coincidence? I don't think so; I believe to this day all the stress from watching her son fall apart, then pull it together, only to fall apart all over again pushed her over the edge. Knowing he was capable of ruining not only his own life, but the lives of those he loved as well was more than she could handle. Loving Jeff had become such a roller coaster ride, and it all wore her down until her life turned in a bad direction.

She soon got to the point she couldn't even be left alone – she became a danger to herself and those around her. Sometimes at night, she would just wander out of her house. During the day, she would get lost while driving, stop and park her car in the middle of the street, and go in whatever building happened to be nearest. One time, that building happened to be the Saline County Courthouse. Dad, the county's Circuit Clerk, saw how disoriented she was and knew we had to do something. Together, the two of us got her license revoked. With the doctor's help, we got her into the local nursing home. It wasn't an easy decision, and she wasn't happy to leave her home, but with Lori and I both working, we knew we couldn't be there all the time.

Meanwhile, Jeff continued down the path of destruction, stealing anything he could get his hands on – even from his own family. He broke into my garage and stole my chainsaw. I noticed it was gone almost immediately and this time, I didn't even entertain any notions it could have been someone other than my brother. My eyes were finally opened enough to realize that when it came to stealing and drugs, Jeff would do anything, even steal from his own family.

I managed to track down the chainsaw at a pawn shop in Marion, along with the seller's name: Jeff Nolen. I didn't shed a single tear, didn't feel the familiar burn of shock that came all those other times when his behavior genuinely surprised me. The numbness had returned to my heart.

When I confronted Jeff, he looked me straight in the eyes. He wore an innocent expression when he said, "I'm so sorry, Jack. I did take that to the pawn shop, but I had no idea it was yours. I bought it off this guy I know. Someone must've broke into your garage and stole it."

I stared at him for a moment, anger bubbling up from my chest into my throat. Did he seriously expect me to believe that? Did he really think I was that dumb? That naïve? I opened my mouth, prepared to scream at him, to tell him I was done with him. But then I closed it again. Furious as I was, I still wasn't ready to shut the door on him yet. Not when I'd seen what he could be. This man standing in front of me, lying right to my face – he wasn't my brother. My brother was buried in there somewhere, somewhere below this monster who took over. I still had this faint glimmer of hope inside that believed my brother could find his way out. He'd done it once before – it could happen again. Right?

Other things disappeared from our home, too. Lori lost a diamond ring, one she'd taken off and laid in her jewelry chest one afternoon while working with her hands. Jeff stopped by to visit, used our bathroom, and a few hours after he was gone, Lori realized the ring was gone, too. Same thing happened with my 9mm pistol. We never tracked down either of those items, but we knew with absolute certainty how they had gotten out of the house. We didn't even bother to confront Jeff this time; it wouldn't have gotten us anywhere. His attitude was, if we couldn't prove he'd done it, then he didn't do it. If he could still lie to me even when I *did* have proof, there was no chance of getting any truth out of him when I didn't.

Dad wasn't safe from his stunts, either. One evening, Jeff called him and asked him and Carol to go out to dinner. Dad was floored by the invitation – Jeff had never done anything like that before. Surprised and admittedly a little skeptical, they decided to go. They had a nice evening together, only to come home and find that someone had tried to break in to their home. Dad knew Jeff had staged the whole thing – luring them out of the house so one of his buddies could attempt to get inside and steal the cash Jeff knew he kept.

My fury overwhelmed me until I could barely bring myself to speak to him. I had always known he was capable of stealing without remorse, but to take every last dime from Mom, running her into debt she couldn't recover from? To bait Dad with the pretense of spending time with him just to get him out of the house in order to try to steal from him? I didn't even recognize this monster who would betray his own family so deeply.

In 2006, Jeff faced charges once again for theft of the jewelry and Mom's money. He was sentenced to four years in prison, of which he served about two. That familiar feeling of guilt-laced relief returned – my brother was off the streets, where he couldn't hurt himself or anyone else for a while. Our family endured two more painful years without him. When he was released, he was only out a few weeks before he was arrested again on possession of a controlled substance.

But this time, I had a not-so-welcome distraction from the worry of my brother and his future. Little did I know, my own health was about to steal the spotlight for a while.

My Brother's Keeper

Chapter Fifteen
A Bump in the Road

In June 2008, I went to Carbondale Memorial Hospital for a routine colonoscopy. Lori came with me, as I would be sedated for the procedure and wouldn't be able to drive myself home.

I dreaded the procedure, as most do, and looked forward to a short, painless experience I would walk away from and not think about again for ten more years. However, things didn't go the way I imagined they would.

I did all the necessary preparations, just as my doctor ordered. I lay back on the exam table, turned over onto my left side, and let the sedatives the doctor injected into the tube in my arm work their magic until I was blissfully unaware of what was happening to me. When I awoke in recovery, the doctor who had performed the procedure stood over me.

"Jack? Are you ready to rejoin us?"

His words barely registered in my head as I tried to focus on his face, unsure of who he was or even who I was at the moment. I blinked several times, trying to push the fog away from my mind. Slowly, I became more alert and the memory of the morning began to resurface. *Hospital…doctor…procedure…* A wave of relief. *It's over.*

"How are you feeling, Jack?"

I swallowed. "Okay."

The doctor nodded, his face serious. "Jack, I have some news to share with you. Are you ready for it?"

I blinked again, allowing the fog to continue to lift as I processed his words. "News?"

"About your procedure."

I squinted. "What is it?"

"Well, Jack, the camera showed a mass in your colon."

Staring at him, I fought through the confusion in my mind to process his statement. "A mass?"

"We won't know without removing it for a biopsy, of course, but...Jack, I've been doing this a long time. It's likely cancerous, and it needs to come out."

The walls began to close in around me. Biopsy? Cancerous?

"I have a surgeon standing by. We can put you back under and remove it *today*. If you – "

"Wait...today? You want to..." I shook my head, still groggy. "No. Not today. I...I need...some time. To process...this. I need to talk to Lori. Where's Lori?" I knew the anesthesia was still lingering so I couldn't think clearly, but I was coherent enough to know I did not want to be put back out and head into surgery just yet. I needed to wake up, get my senses about me. I needed to discuss the situation with Lori and my kids.

And that's exactly what I did. When Lori and I left the doctor's office that day, we made an appointment to meet with the surgeon the following week.

The car ride home was quiet, Lori and I both lost in our own thoughts. Cancer? I'd had no symptoms, no indications anything was wrong. I left my house that morning, ready to get the procedure over with and get on with my day, going about life as usual. I never imagined the doctor would find something wrong.

"We'll get through this." Lori's voice interrupted my thoughts. "You'll have the surgery. They'll remove it, and everything will be just fine." I wasn't sure who she was trying harder to convince – me, or herself.

"I know it will," I assured her. And I meant it. Strange – as hard as it was to swallow the news I had cancer, I had a sense of peace about it all. Somehow, I felt calm. *Okay, God. It's in Your hands. I trust You. But...there must be something You're trying to show me in all of this. What is it?*

I relayed the news to Tiffany and Jackson that evening. Lori sat next to me on the couch and held my hand as I told them what the doctor had told me just hours earlier, though it seemed like days.

Tiffany paced our living room floor, clutching her two-year-old son, Gavin. Her eyes filled with tears she quickly blinked away. "It's not fair," she said finally, shaking her head. "It doesn't...

why? Why us? Why you?"

"Hey." I stood up from the couch and closed the distance between us. When I stood in front of her, Gavin reached his little hands up toward me, and I scooped him out of her arms. A fleeting, unwelcome thought invaded my mind as his big eyes searched mine. *I won't be able to watch him grow up.* I shook my head, forcing it to the back of my mind. "It's going to be okay. I'm going to be okay. This is just…a little bump in the road, you know?"

My daughter sighed and pulled her arms to her chest, hugging herself.

"This kind of thing happens all the time. The surgery is very common. The doctors there are good. They know what they're doing. They'll take care of me."

Tiffany nodded, again blinking back tears. I pulled her to me and held her close, letting her hug me tightly. As she clung to me, I looked over to the recliner where Jackson sat. I couldn't help but see myself in him – the same look I knew I wore when I was in deep concentration. His furrowed eyebrows, his eyes locked on the wall in front of him. He hadn't said a word yet. I knew he was thinking it through before he responded; that's the way he always handled things. After a few moments, he stood to his feet, then crossed the room to join us. I pulled away from Tiffany just enough to let him step in. I soon felt Lori's hands on my back, and the five of us just stood there, all wrapped up in one big hug, until Gavin began to squirm to let us know he was done being squished by us.

Jackson grabbed my shoulder. "You're right, Dad: it'll be okay. God's got this."

I smiled, my heart soaring with pride at the young man my son was becoming. "I know He does, buddy."

I had a fishing trip scheduled for just two weeks away – something I looked forward to every year. My buddy from work, Wade, and I went to Minnesota every summer and spent a week there in a cabin, doing nothing but fishing from sunup to sundown. The lake was so peaceful and calm. Any stress melted away while Wade and I sat in that boat, casting our line out over and over again. I wasn't going to miss that trip, but I wanted to let Wade know what was going on. The next morning, I called him.

The phone only rang once before Wade's cheerful voice greeted me. "Hey, Jack. What do you know?"

I took a deep breath, trying to decide how to say it. *Just come out with it.* "I have cancer."

Silence. "You...you what?"

"I have cancer." Wade listened wordlessly as I relayed the events of the day before.

When I finished, he let out a long sigh. "Wow. I...I don't know what to say. I...I'm shocked. What can I do? What do you need?"

I swallowed. "Prayer. Just prayer."

"You got it, buddy. And hey, I'll call the lodge, cancel our reservation. Maybe we can – "

"What? No. We're not canceling our trip."

Silence again. "Jack, are you...don't you think you..."

"No. I'm going. This...this may be the last time I ever get to..." I choked, unable to finish my sentence.

"No, it won't be," Wade answered, his voice firm and steady. "Don't even talk like that. You're going to make it through this." I nodded, knowing he couldn't see me, but I couldn't find the words.

"Listen, maybe we should – "

"We're going on this trip. We...we just have to. A couple more weeks with this won't change a thing. We're going fishing. I'll deal with this when we get back."

More silence. Finally, Wade sighed. "Okay, buddy. Then let's go do some fishing."

The next week, Lori and I met with the surgeon, who echoed what the doctor had told me after my colonoscopy: the mass needed to come out. They would remove it, along with the surrounding tissue and lymph nodes for testing. We scheduled the surgery for the first week in July.

For three weeks, I went about my life as I always had. Wade and I went on our fishing trip, and we laughed and talked like nothing had changed. On the inside, I felt different somehow. Knowing what lurked inside my body put a slight damper on the joy the lake usually brought. But as I sat out in that boat one evening, watching the sky turn various shades of pink, orange, and purple over the water as the sun made its descent, I was filled with that same peace I'd had in the car on the way home from my colonoscopy. For just a moment, I looked out in awe at the absolute beauty in front of me, and I felt He'd made it just for me. And I knew I was going to be okay. The same God who made that beautiful sunset was the One who had me in His arms. What did I have to be afraid of? *Thank You, God, for loving me. I don't know why You do – I definitely don't deserve it. But thank You. Thank You for loving me, for knowing me, for having a purpose for me. I trust You.*

As my surgery drew near, that peace remained. I wasn't angry with my circumstances and I wasn't scared of the outcome. In fact, I was still just so grateful – grateful it was me and not my wife, or my kids, or my grandkids. God had already brought me through so much and I knew, I just knew, that He would bring me through all this, too.

I woke up early the morning of my surgery, expecting waves of anxiety to finally come. But they didn't. Whenever butterflies would start to flutter in my stomach, I prayed. *God, I trust You. Please be with me and with the doctors throughout this. Please comfort my family and bring them peace.* I was still repeating that prayer when the anesthesiologist injected my arm and put me into a deep sleep.

When I awoke and the anesthesia wore off enough that I could understand the doctor's words, he told me they had removed almost half my colon in order to eliminate the cancerous part. The surrounding tissue and lymph nodes would be tested to determine if the cancer had spread.

As it turned out, it had. At my follow-up appointment, my doctor delivered the bad news: they found cancer cells in a lymph node and determined that the cancer was in stage three, which would require chemotherapy treatments.

Hearing my doctor say "stage three cancer" was a blow, with each word seeming to punch me in the stomach. I had imagined the way that follow-up appointment would go – my doctor would smile at me and tell me they had gotten all the cancer, and

I could put the nightmare behind me and move on with my life. I sat in shock, absorbing the information, as Lori sat beside me and swiped at the tears that spilled over onto her cheeks. *Okay, God. This...is a curveball.*

"You won't begin chemotherapy until you have fully recovered from your surgery," the doctor continued, his tone even and methodical. "You will receive a Catha-port, which we will use to administer your treatment. We will all meet as a team – me, you, and the oncologist – to determine the frequency and duration of treatments."

Lori and I rode home in silence once again, just as we had done the day of my colonoscopy, the day the roller coaster ride had begun. I couldn't believe the ride was still going, and it wasn't over yet. Judging from the continuous tears rolling down her face, I could tell Lori couldn't believe it, either.

God, I know You work all things together for our good. I just...I'm having trouble seeing the good in all this. But I know You see what I can't see. And I trust You. I know I've already asked You for so much, but now I'm asking You for strength. For peace. Not just for me, but for Lori and my family. We're going to need it now more than ever.

Healing from my surgery took longer than I imagined it would. Lori took on the role of nurse, making sure I was comfortable all the time. I grew frustrated when I couldn't get around as easily and as quickly as I wanted, but if Lori ever got tired of waiting on me hand and foot, she never showed it. She was a saint, buzzing around me all the time, bringing me anything I needed or wanted, sitting and talking to me when I knew she had other things she needed to do, and giving me time to myself when she could tell I just wanted to be alone.

Day by day, I regained my strength. But while the biggest part of me was relieved by my reclaimed independence, a smaller part was filled with a new sense of dread of what was to come. I knew my recovery meant my treatments would begin.

By the end of August, I felt much more like myself again. The day I went in to receive my Catha-port, I felt healthier than I had in a long time. It didn't seem right, feeling so strong when inside my body lurked a silent killer working against me.

My first treatment would begin on Monday, September 3,

2008, at eight o'clock in the morning. As per the plan created by the team, I would sit at the clinic all day, until about three o'clock, receiving chemotherapy and other drugs through an IV into my port. Once the bags were empty, I would leave with a fanny pack that contained a pump and more chemotherapy drugs in it. I would wear that fanny pack for the rest of the day and all through the night, hanging it on my bed post, so that I would get a continuous flow through the Catha-port. On Tuesday morning, I was to be back at the clinic for another full day of treatment, just like the day before, and again leave with the fanny pack. This time, the fanny pack would be charged with enough drugs in it to last until about four o'clock in the afternoon on Wednesday, when I would go back to the clinic so they could remove the pump. This would continue every other week for six months, giving me twelve treatments in all.

One positive thing about my treatments was that I could do them in Harrisburg, and my doctor assured me I would be able to drive myself to and from the treatment. The last thing I wanted was to inconvenience my wife or anyone else in my family by taking up three days out of their already busy schedules. I hated to ask someone to drive me somewhere three days a week, and I didn't expect or even want someone to have to sit there with me for seven full hours, twice a week.

That first full day of treatment was brutal – not because it was painful, but just so incredibly boring. I'd never been one to sit still for very long in my life. I could hardly sit through a movie without getting up and walking around. To sit there all day, watching those big bags trickle drip-by-drip into my system, was nothing short of torture. I had told Lori she didn't even have to come, but was I ever glad when she came and sat with me throughout most of the day.

As the doctor warned, I felt a little sick after the first week of treatments. When I drove myself to turn in that fanny pack Wednesday afternoon, I felt like I'd just had the flu – tired, with a little headache and some nausea. I stayed in that condition for a couple days, but by the weekend, I felt pretty good again. I was grateful for the week off and dreaded going back to repeat the process.

But if I thought that first week of treatment was grueling, it was nothing compared to the weeks that followed. The chemotherapy's effects kicked in during that first week, but they only seemed to intensify with each passing week. The further into the treatments I got, the longer it seemed to take to recover. It wore on my immune system, making me so weak that in December, my doctor ordered me to skip a treatment before Christmas. I didn't want to, as I already had my completion date circled on the calendar and I was counting down to the day – the last thing I wanted was a setback. It did, however, allow me to feel a little better for Christmas, although I have to admit I don't remember much about the holiday. The chemo affected my mind as well, making me forget conversations and things that happened. Doctors refer to it as "chemo fog."

I could see in my dad's eyes how hard it was for him to see me go through cancer. It seemed to physically age him, watching his son suffer. But he always stayed positive, always did whatever he could to keep me smiling. He stopped by every time I did my treatments, bringing me a snack he thought I might like or a newspaper or magazine to help pass the time. He sat with me for a while at every treatment and called me every single night to see how I was feeling.

I actually felt as well as I possibly could have under the circumstances, and it was mainly due to my wife. When the chemo made me nauseous, she did everything she could to make sure I ate, fixing me anything I asked for. She made sure I was as comfortable as I could be. If I had work to do, she propped me up on the couch and set up my computer for me. If I had somewhere to go, she helped me get wherever I needed to be. Though I could drive myself, it wasn't easy trying to get ready with a fanny pack full of poison buckled around my waist. When I lost my strength, she *became* my strength. I relied on her for everything.

My kids were there as well. Tiffany and Jackson checked on me constantly, helping however they could. Even my grandson, Gavin, took care of me. When I lay on the couch or the bed, feeling really sick from the treatment, he'd slide in beside me and snuggle up against me, lying there until he went to sleep. At his young age, he still realized something was wrong with his grandpa and just wanted to be beside me.

Jackson had just begun his senior year of high school when I took my first treatment. Football was a big part of his world, and he was proud to be the starting center on the team. He had practice after school on the day I started my treatments, but he was worried about how I would do with it and asked his coach if he could be excused from practice to be with me. "You can miss practice," the coach told him, "but you won't be starting in the next game."

Jackson missed anyway. After thinking about his coach's words, he decided football wasn't as important as family, and if it meant he had to choose, then he no longer wanted to play. He loved football and had been dedicated to the sport and all the training that went along with it for his entire high school career. But the next morning, he walked into his coach's office and turned in his gear. He never looked back. He actually got the chance to play again in college, but by that time, he had already set his goal on becoming a police officer, and he wasn't going to let anything deter him from that. He had a full class load and playing football would have meant lessening that load to allow time for the practice schedule. He made his decision alone, with no input from Lori or me. While I hated to see him give up something he loved, I was proud of the man he was becoming, proud to see his priorities in the right place.

With the help of my family, I got through those difficult months of chemo. I don't know how I would have made it without my wife, my kids, and Dad and Carol. My brother-in-law, Terry, was also there for me, sticking close by my side and taking care of me whenever and however he could. I know my mom would have been there for me, too, if she could have been – but with her deteriorating mental health, I chose to keep her in the dark as best I could so she didn't even know I was sick. I didn't want to give her something else to worry about.

In February 2009, I finally finished my treatments. I'll never forget the day I got to turn that fanny pack pump back in for the last time. I wanted to leave there with it tied to the bumper of my truck and drag it around until there was nothing left. The winter had been so hard on me, and the treatments had left me really weak.

But while I looked forward to getting back to the normal I had once known, life had other plans for me.

Just days after finishing my final treatment, I slipped on some ice and took a hard fall. My body was already weak from the chemo, but especially my bad back – I had already undergone three surgeries to repair ruptured discs in my life. I stood up and walked away from my fall, relieved I didn't break any bones, but I knew I had done some damage to my back. Something just didn't feel right. I tried my best to ignore the pain; I was done with doctors for a while. When the pain persisted, I shook it off. *You're not a kid anymore*, I reasoned. *A fall is going to leave you feeling a little sorer than it used to.* I did my best to ignore it and go about my business. *It'll go away on its own. Eventually.*

A couple weeks later, I tried to do some work in my yard outside when I felt a tearing sensation in my back. I froze, unable to move. As it turned out, I ruptured two more discs. This time, I couldn't ignore the pain. I couldn't take more than a couple steps at a time without having to stop, doubled over in agony.

Fortunately, my surgeon in St. Louis was able to get me in quickly. He had told me before that if I re-injured it I would have to have it fused. X-rays showed I had ruptured the L4-L5 disc again, as well as the L5-S1.

I was frustrated, naturally. Just when I thought the roller coaster was heading back up the hill, it took a sudden dive. It would have been tempting to want to give up, to shake my fist at God and yell. *Why is this happening to me? Haven't I been through enough?* But amazingly, even with my new injury, God gave me peace. Instead of letting me wallow in my own self-pity, He provided me with a sense of calm. I pictured that sunset and remembered He was in control. I was actually grateful again that it was me going through it all, rather than someone else in my family. I knew if my wife was in my shoes, I wouldn't have been capable of being half the support, half the nurse, that she was for me. I knew how hard it was for my dad, watching me go through everything, and I was so thankful I didn't have to be in his shoes, watching my kids or grandkids go through that kind of pain and heartache. I didn't feel sorry for myself, and I didn't want anyone else to feel sorry for me, either. God let me know from the beginning He would take care of me through it all. Instead of searching for the *why*, I spent a lot of time praying, asking God what He wanted to show me in all of it.

In May 2009, I went in for an eight-hour surgery to remove bone from my hip, which would be used to fuse my back. This meant being cut open in the stomach, as they fuse from the front side, which required an even longer recovery time – about six months.

I've never felt more helpless than I did after that surgery. I was like a baby all over again, needing assistance with all the small tasks I'd taken for granted, like bending down to pick up something as small as a pencil. The pain, post-surgery, was excruciating at times. But again, my family stepped up to the plate, taking care of me in every possible way. Lori never once complained as she did anything and everything I needed or wanted. My kids continued to look after me and make sacrifices for my comfort. My dad never failed to call me every day and stopped by the house regularly to see if I needed anything or just to keep me company for a while.

Between the previous surgery to remove the cancer, the chemo treatments, and then the back surgery, I was down for a little over a year. All of the chaos in my own life provided an escape from my brother's problems and the anger that burned inside of me when I thought about the way he had betrayed our family, especially our parents. He was locked up after his arrest for possession of a controlled substance during part of that time, as his bail amount was set so high he couldn't get himself out. Dad often told me during his visits that Jeff asked about me and how I was doing, and only then would I realize I had gone a day or sometimes several without losing sleep at night, worrying about my little brother. He knew everything that was going on with me but wasn't able to be there the way the rest of my family was, and that was okay. God put so many people in my path that stepped into my life in a big way, overwhelming me with love and support throughout that year. There was never a day that passed that someone wasn't there to lift me up and help me get through it.

God assured me from the day of that colonoscopy He was in control of my life and my situation. I knew He would bring something good from it all, and He did that through the relationships He provided for me during that time. And it wasn't just my family. He built relationships with dear friends who became closer than brothers to me, including Stan and Wade.

Stan had been one of my best friends since childhood. He had been there for me through so much, and that year was no exception. Wade and I became friends a little later in life, working together at Sahara Coal and again at Long-Airdox. We had grown close as adults, but my health issues only brought us closer. I knew both of them loved me, and they knew I loved them, but like most grown men, we weren't comfortable expressing that affection. But during that year, for the first time, they told me they loved me. Now, it's commonplace in our conversations to include those words. Today, both of those men remain like brothers to me. The relationships I built with them, especially during that time, have and will last a lifetime.

God never promised that our walk in this life would be easy. But in the midst of trials, of pain, He puts people in our path who can help us through it all. I am so thankful for my wife and all she sacrificed for me. I'm thankful for my children and grandchildren and all the love and help they gave me. I'm thankful for my brother-in-law and my good friends who became closer than blood and offered the support I needed to get through that difficult time.

I thought I trusted God before my bout with cancer, but I never fully understood what it meant to trust Him until I found myself facing my own mortality. Feeling vulnerable like that, relying on other people so heavily every day, only taught me to rely on Him that much more. Without Him, we are helpless. We just sometimes forget to recognize it until something like cancer comes along and reminds us.

Chapter Sixteen
A Devastating Loss

Life, as it always does, moved on. That year quickly became nothing more than a blur in my mind. I was so thankful for my health and all the blessings God had shown me, all around me, that it took my focus off of my brother for a time. But deep down, I still struggled with the anger I held in my heart toward him. I could get past the fact he stole from my wife and me. But Mom? And Dad? I would never understand that.

The court had ordered Jeff to pay back every cent he had stolen from our mom. I was her point of attorney, and Jeff actually had the nerve to contact me to ask him for help. "Come on, Jack," he pleaded. "I'm in over my head. Can't you talk to the judge? Ask them to relieve me of that? I need a break."

I waited for that familiar tug, that compulsion to help him out of whatever jam he'd gotten himself into. But this time, it wasn't there. My anger was just too strong. "Jeff, you…" I took a deep breath. "You've had more breaks than I can count, little brother. I'm sorry…I can't help you this time."

He hung up the phone without saying goodbye. I expected tears to sting my eyes, but they never came. It seemed my eyes were drying up.

In 2010, Jeff was arrested again for possession of meth. His 2008 arrest for possession of a controlled substance was still dragging through the court system as well, and in August 2011, he was sentenced for both. He was handed three years for the controlled substance charge, along with four and a half more for the meth.

Time and stress began to take a bigger toll on our dad. He never gave up on Jeff, but even he felt the same relief I did when Jeff was in jail. He still worried about him constantly, but it was a different kind of worry – at least when he was in jail, he didn't worry about where he was and what he was doing. It feels strange to admit our family almost preferred my brother being in jail, but it was true. He had food to eat. He didn't have access to street drugs. And there was always the possibility that this time, it would straighten him out. We'd seen it happen before – it could happen again. And maybe this time, it would stick.

But something was wrong with Dad, and it was more than just his worries. He didn't say anything at first, but he didn't have to – I knew something was wrong. He was sick.

I just didn't know how sick.

Early in 2011, Dad was diagnosed with melanoma.

Of course we were all scared. Memories of my own battle with cancer returned, fresh once again. I didn't want to see my dad go through the nightmare I'd experienced. But the doctors were optimistic. And this was my *dad* we were talking about – the closest thing to Superman I'd ever known. If anyone could beat this, he could.

He went through two surgeries and his prognosis was pretty good – a full body scan prior to the second surgery showed only one hot spot in the lymph nodes near his shoulder. A few weeks after the surgery, the doctor ordered some scans. Dad was strong. A fighter. He felt pretty good, and we expected these scans to tell us he was cancer-free and this nightmare was behind us.

But there was something else we didn't know. It wasn't good, but because God *is* good, He found a way to tell us what we need to hear.

One of the scans accidentally got a portion of Dad's head in one of the angles. A brain tumor showed up.

The doctor from Vanderbilt called him the Friday before Memorial Day weekend. Dad, Carol, and I drove to Nashville to meet with him in person. We looked over the scan in more detail while the doctor talked to us about the tumor.

Dad listened carefully. Then, in his typical no-nonsense fashion, he held his head high and looked at the doctor. "All right, don't sugarcoat it. Tell it to me straight. What does this mean?"

I can still picture that doctor's face, can still hear his gravelly voice when he looked directly into Dad's eyes, sighed, and said,

"You've got a few months left, tops."

Suddenly, the walls in the room seemed to close in around me. The doctor continued to speak, giving my dad options, things he could do to prolong his time left. A treatment plan. But I didn't hear any of it. My ears rang so loudly. I could see the doctor's lips moving, but no sound seemed to come out.

This can't be happening. God, please, tell me this isn't real. I can't lose my dad. Not yet.

I managed to pull it together enough to listen as Dad agreed to try radiation treatments. Carol and I took him to meet with the oncologist, who explained the radiation process. He was upbeat, very optimistic. He told us the radiation would make Dad feel tired, but despite that warning, I was sure my dad would do well with the treatments. He had to. He *had* to.

A few months? That doctor didn't know my dad. And doctors were wrong about that kind of thing all the time. My dad would be one of those miracle stories you hear, the kind where people say things like, "The doctor told him he only had three months to live. But he went through treatments, and six months later, his scans came back clear!" I could actually *hear* myself telling people that very thing one day down the road, giving God the glory for healing my dad.

I don't really know what I expected from those first radiation treatments. I heard the oncologist when he said Dad would feel tired and groggy, and I was a grown man – old enough to realize that unlike my childhood beliefs, my dad was not invincible. But even after all those years, he was still my hero, and for good reason – my dad truly was the strongest man I knew.

But 'tired and groggy' was a gross understatement. After only three treatments, my dad was bedridden. Deathly pale. Those three days had aged him tremendously, leaving him frail and weak.

I sat next to him on his bed, trying to be the cheerleader I thought he needed. "It'll get easier. Your body will adjust to this. You just have to keep going, keep fighting."

Dad shook his head. In his frail condition, even that small movement seemed difficult. "I can't keep doing this, Jack."

My heart rate quickened. "You have to."

"No, I don't. And I won't."

We stared at each other. I searched for the right words to say to convince him not to give up. But before I found them, he spoke again. "Look at me, son. I'm...this is killing me faster than the cancer will."

Tears filled my eyes and spilled over onto my cheeks. "Don't say that."

Dad reached over and took my hand. "Jack, I...I'm not scared to die. I know where I'm going."

Tears gushed faster. I knew my dad had found Jesus years earlier, but it didn't bring me any comfort at that moment. "That's not the part I'm worried about."

I sobbed, unable to bring myself to say anymore, to tell him how lost I would be without him. But I didn't have to. He knew. He opened his arms so I could fall onto his chest, like a little boy who needed his daddy.

We all knew his time was short. For the next three weeks, I spent every minute I possibly could at his house. But on June 24, I had to leave town for Milwaukee. There were some work meetings there that weekend and the beginning of the following week and my dad insisted I go. I wanted to talk to my boss, to explain the situation and get out of it, but Dad wouldn't hear of it. "I'll be fine, Jack. It's just a few days. Go. You have to take care of your job."

And so I did. I called every night around eight thirty, knowing Carol would get him settled into bed at nine o'clock. He sounded okay on the phone those first couple evenings, but a little pit formed in my stomach with each passing day, and I knew something wasn't right. On Monday, June 27, I called earlier in the day to check on him. He didn't sound like himself – he was winded and his words seemed labored.

As soon as I hung up the phone, I called Lori. "I just talked to Dad. He...doesn't sound good."

"I'll go up there and check on him, see if Carol needs anything."

"Thank you." It was yet another time I was incredibly grateful for my wife. Knowing she and Jackson would be there brought a little peace to my mind, but not much. They went to visit around six o'clock, and then I called back at my usual eight thirty. He did sound a little better than he had that afternoon, but after only about ten minutes, he said he was getting tired and was going to head to bed a little early.

At eight fifty, he got up to go to the bathroom. As he headed down the hall, he collapsed.

Shortly after nine o'clock on June 27, 2011, I got the phone call that would forever change my life.

My heart shattered as I listened to a family friend break the news – my dad, my hero, was gone. The coroner determined he had a massive heart attack and died right there in the hallway where he collapsed that night. A new hole burst open in my chest, but this time, there was no hope anything could ever fill it.

I packed up, called my boss to inform him what had happened, and checked out of the hotel. It was around ten o'clock when I filled up my gas tank and headed out for the seven-hour drive home.

Driving alone through the night gave me a lot of time to reflect and remember things. It was like a seven-hour roller coaster ride, emotionally, as I went from devastated to grateful and everything in between. I sobbed heavily, unable to imagine a life without my dad. At the same time, when I pictured him running into Jesus's arms, happy and cancer-free, I smiled. I remembered all the hunting trips, all the rides next to him in his police car. I didn't have many good memories that didn't include him somehow. I was so thankful for the time I had with him, thankful that God had chosen him to be my father. I was thankful for my wife and the fact that she and Jackson were there for him.

Jackson. My heart broke all over again when I thought of my son and how he must be feeling. My dad wasn't just my hero; he was Jackson's, too. He was my son's inspiration to become a police officer, and he was going to Greenville University to be just that. I hated I wasn't there to hold him at that moment. I felt helpless, so many hours away when my family needed me. And God knew how much I needed them.

I needed Jeff, too. Did he even know yet? I imagined him weeping in his cell. Would he think about the old days? Would he feel regret for the choices he made, for the stress he'd brought upon our dad?

Jeff trudged into the funeral home in chains and shackles before the actual funeral service – he wasn't allowed to attend. Carol met him there so he could have those few minutes to say his final goodbyes to our father.

I've never been to a funeral like my dad's. He had told us after his diagnosis that he didn't want a sad funeral; he wanted a celebration of life. And that's exactly what it was. There were funny stories, stories of how Dad had inspired others. Jackson even managed to hold himself together to get up and speak. There was so much laughter and so many tears. Dad was cremated and his ashes were transported in a state police car to the cemetery for burial. When the Illinois State Police Honor Guard went through their cadence and the bagpipes played at the cemetery, I wept for so many reasons. I missed him so much already. I missed him so much I physically ached all over. Yet I was proud of the legacy he left behind, proud of the tribute we'd paid him – I knew that day was exactly how he would have wanted it.

My emotions overwhelmed me. Not having my brother there with me while I looked at my father for the last time did something inside of me. I wanted Jeff there, needed him there to lean on. But he wasn't next to me. In the midst of my grief, anger stirred. I couldn't help but blame Jeff a little for Dad's heart attack. Everything he stood for, everything he spent his life fighting against, was ripped apart by his own son. Maybe he didn't directly cause Dad's physical deterioration, but I knew the stress he put him through couldn't have helped it, either.

I hated losing him, hated the way he was stolen from me so quickly. He just went down so *fast*. It felt like one day, the doctors were telling us this devastating news, and before I could even process it, could even truly prepare myself for what was coming, he was gone. Yet, in the midst of the devastating loss of my life, I found reasons to thank God. I was so worried about him suffering from the tumor and the treatments, and because of the way the events played out, he didn't have to. I will also be forever grateful his last words to me were, "I love you." The last thing he ever heard me say was, "Bye, Dad. I love you, too." We never left each other or hung up the phone without telling each other we loved each other; from the time we were little, my dad made it a point to tell us how he felt as often as he could.

Dad's death signaled an attitude change in me. My dad wasn't there anymore, and mentally, my mom wasn't either. And as much as it hurt to admit it, my brother was gone, too. The last several years had been such a whirlwind, such a wild ride with Jeff, filled with twists and turns into some really dark places. With Dad's death came an eerie stillness, and for the first time in years, I was forced to really sit down and *think*.

I heard Dad's words in my head over and over again: "I just try to get Jeff to the corner. It's up to him to turn it." Despite all he'd seen through the years in his line of work, when it came to Jeff, he remained determined. Optimistic, even.

But after numerous long, exhausting trips to the corner, my efforts were beginning to feel like a waste of time. Any hope I'd ever have my real brother back again was all but gone. For years, I'd prayed constantly. Lost sleep. Begged him to change, begged God to change him. Cleaned up his messes. Helped him find jobs. And for what? To be constantly let down? Lied to? Stolen from?

All my life, I had been my brother's keeper. And I still loved him, still worried about him, still desperately wished for what we'd once had. But something inside of me shifted, and I found myself assuming a new role: my family's protector. And unfortunately, the main thing I felt compelled to protect them from was Jeff. His addiction not only destroyed him, it destroyed everyone and everything in his path. Our parents. His marriages. A stable home life for his daughters. And I had to admit, I'd let him affect my own marriage and family. I allowed him to come in to our home, time and again, even after he'd stolen from me, from Lori...even from Tiffany. Thankfully, my family was understanding and supportive enough to keep giving him those same chances I did.

I often found myself frustrated by my unanswered prayers throughout that time. Why wasn't God fixing him? Why wasn't he changing him, making him into the man I knew He created him to be? But finally, after all my family had endured, I got to a place where I could hear God's voice. I realized that though God could have changed Jeff, that's just not the way He works. God will never force someone to do His will. He loved my brother and didn't want to see him lost to the addiction. He put people in Jeff's life, gave him opportunities and resources in his path to help him make the change he needed. But at the end of the day, it was ultimately Jeff's decision. That's what *free will* is all about.

When my eyes and my heart were finally open to this, it also hit me that God knows exactly what we need before we even realize we're in a situation where we need anything. All those times my brother had been arrested and taken to jail seemed like such a blow to me, to our family, at the time. But what was the alternative? For him to slip through the cracks of the justice system, running the streets, becoming more and more out of control until he died of an overdose? What if him being locked up kept him from hurting himself or someone else?

And as strange as it sounds, I believe Jeff being in jail was something I sometimes needed, too. Only eight months after Dad died, the Leap Day Tornado hit Harrisburg, destroying homes and businesses and claiming lives in its path. Dad and Carol's house was severely damaged. Luckily, Carol was safe, staying in Florida with her sister...but that left my family and me to take care of it. By that time, Tiffany had three kids of her own, and Jackson was away in Greenville, finishing college. With all the stress and chaos, I had one less worry on my plate. I didn't have to worry if Jeff was okay, if my doors and windows were locked, if he would ransack Dad and Carol's empty, damaged house. It was a relief to know for the time being, while life tossed other curveballs my way, I didn't have to lose sleep worrying about my brother.

But I never stopped praying for him. I'd seen what God could do, what he'd already done in my own life. I'd been through so much heartache and loss, yet through it all, I repeatedly saw God and His blessings around me. I saw Him in my grandchildren's laughter. I saw Him in my wife, who stood by my side through all my ups and downs. I saw Him in my kids, in the fierce love He instilled inside of me for them and the unconditional love they gave back when I was at my lowest points.

And I'd seen the work He'd begun in Jeff not long ago. Like

in all of us, His work in my brother was unfinished. He was broken. He'd turned his back on God, seemingly forgetting what he'd found at the church altar that Sunday morning. But I knew what my brother had experienced there was real. And I knew if Jeff asked Him to, He'd pick up right where He left off before Jeff left the path intended for his life.

So as he neared the end of his prison sentence, I found myself asking God the same thing I'd been begging for throughout the years: *God, please let this be it. Let this time in prison be just what he needed to finally turn that corner he's been to so many times before. We've all been through so much, lost so much. Please, just let me have my little brother back for good.*

My Brother's Keeper

Chapter Seventeen
The Apple and the Tree

In June 2013, Jeff was released from jail. Ironically enough, his entrance back into society happened right around the time Jackson graduated from Greenville University with a criminal justice degree. He was hired on as a police officer in Edwardsville, Illinois, and sent to the police academy.

Jeff had a special place in his heart for Jackson. He loved his three girls so much and loved my daughter, Tiffany, as well. But when we found out our second would be a boy, Jeff fell in love in a different way. He bought him gifts while Lori was pregnant – hunting stuff, mostly. Unfortunately, by the time Jackson was old enough to really get to know his uncle, Jeff was far into his addiction. My kids never truly got to meet the man I once knew, the man I desperately wished would re-emerge from underneath the demon that held him so tightly. Even still, Jackson especially felt a connection with Jeff. He, like I did, had high hopes for a complete recovery.

From the time he was young, Jackson loved the Lord with everything he had. He even became a preacher and worked as a fill-in pastor at local churches. He prayed for Jeff constantly. When I would become discouraged and sometimes fully exasperated, it was Jackson who refused to give up. "It's not too late, Dad. You never know – maybe today will be the day. Maybe there's something I can say or do today that will help him turn his life around." My son, the eternal optimist. One of Jeff's biggest cheerleaders.

I believe the prison system has its benefits. For addicts like Jeff, it can help them re-acclimate to society when their sentence is up. It can get them into a halfway house, help them get a minimum wage job. Jeff had taken advantage of the program after his release from prison, living in a halfway house and taking a job washing dishes at a restaurant in Carbondale, Illinois.

Jeff didn't waste any time before he began dating a new woman, Shayla. I didn't know much about her and as far as I was concerned, neither did Jeff, having only known her a few weeks, but he really liked her from the day he met her. I wasn't sure how I felt about that – I wanted him to concentrate on work and just trying to get back into the real world. But I tried to stay hopeful. With a new job and a new girlfriend, he seemed happy.

But one night, on his way home from work, he fell asleep behind the wheel and ran off the road. He went down into a really deep ditch, rolling his vehicle several times, and he wasn't wearing a seatbelt. Air Evac flew him to Evansville, Indiana, where he was kept in a drug-induced coma for three days while they treated internal injuries, as well as back, hip, and head wounds.

Lori, Tiffany, and I went straight to the hospital when we found out about the accident. By the time we arrived, he was already in a coma, but Shayla was there with him and she told us the tests showed he had no drugs in his system. He claimed he simply fell asleep and while I wanted so badly to believe that, I couldn't help but have my doubts. Even if blood tests had shown drugs, would Shayla have admitted that to us? My instincts told me no.

When he was out of the coma and able to have visitors, I went back to the hospital. I stood next to his bed, looking down at his bandaged head, his bruised face, the tubes running to different places of his body. "You gave us quite a scare, little brother."

He managed a smile. "Yeah, I guess I did."

"What happened?"

Swallowing, he lifted one shoulder. "I was worn out. I haven't gotten much sleep lately – I've been working all the time. I...just fell asleep."

I searched his eyes, looking for any hint that he may be hiding something from me. But who was I kidding? Jeff was and had always been the best liar I knew. He could stare me in the face and swear the sky was neon green, and when those innocent eyes looked into mine, I'd believe every word he said. Almost.

There was a time I would have believed him. I would have believed anything he told me, simply because I wanted to. There's so much power in that, in wanting to believe something. It can make you have faith in some far-fetched ideas. But Jeff had lied to me so many times, and like the villagers in the story of the boy who cried wolf, I had lost my faith in his word. He may very well have fallen asleep that night, with no drug-related assistance. But with his track record, I couldn't believe that. As much as I wanted to – as much as I wanted to believe since he'd only been out of prison a short time, he'd do things differently this time – my gut told me otherwise.

He spent five days in intensive care before spending eight more days in the hospital; he turned fifty years old while lying in that bed. He probably should have stayed longer than he did, but because he had no insurance, he got the minimum stay. He was lucky to survive, but ultimately came out relatively unscathed – other than the fact that he lost his job.

Just over a month after leaving the hospital, Jeff announced his engagement to Shayla. I gave him the best congratulations I could muster, but inside, my stomach churned. This was too fast; he still barely knew her. He wasn't ready to jump into this kind of commitment. With so many broken marriages behind him, why would he jump into another one? Why wouldn't he wait, give himself some time to get his life back on track?

Despite the doubts that plagued my mind, Jackson soothed me. Or at least he attempted to. "You never know, Dad. Maybe he's really found the one after all these years of mistakes; maybe he'll get it right this time. Maybe this will be a new start for him, a clean slate. God can use this woman, this marriage, to help Jeff get on track." And with that positive mindset, Jackson agreed to marry Jeff and Shayla.

As hard as it was on me to be let down time after time, it was even harder to see it happen to my son. On a cool October day in the local park, Jackson stood proud under a shelter, ready to marry his uncle. But when Jeff stumbled toward us, high on pills and half-drunk, I could actually see Jackson deflate. So much for that new start, that clean slate.

Jackson went on with the ceremony as planned, but there was a change in his attitude after the wedding. He had to distance himself from the situation. He continued to pray for Jeff, but even he was becoming discouraged. There seemed to be little hope for my brother.

Shayla had a house on the north side of town and Jeff moved in with her. But he still hadn't found a job.

In our area, Jeff's job options were thin. He had been given chance after chance through the years. So many people were willing to give him a shot, if for no other reason than they knew my dad or me. But his chances were running out. In my mind, that should have been enough reason to try to get his life on track again. But Jeff's mind – or at least, Jeff's mind while controlled by drugs – didn't work that way. No job? Then he'd turn to crime.

And that's exactly what he did. In December – just two months after the wedding – both Jeff and Shayla were arrested. They were charged with delivering a controlled substance, busted for selling drugs to an undercover cop. Both were taken to jail, where they spent a few days before some of Shayla's family raised enough money to get her out. As soon as she was free, she got enough money together to get Jeff out two days later.

By that time, Jeff was *tired* of jail. He had spent approximately ten of the last fifteen years locked up, and he didn't want to go back. Their case drug through the court system, but it seemed sure when they were finally sentenced, he would go back. So, he did what he had to do to get out of it: he agreed to work with law enforcement. He would provide them with information – buyers, sellers, users – in exchange for a reduced sentence for both Shayla and him. He even worked undercover for them, making several buys.

But working with police didn't change him. He went right back to his familiar patterns, including theft. As always, he left no proof. I always joked, if you could call it that, that he was on the "varsity team" of stealing. When things started disappearing around town – from local businesses, from people's homes – it usually had Jeff's name all over it. Except it *didn't*. Jeff was a master of stealing without leaving a trace. He brought a whole new meaning to the phrase, "learn from your mistakes." Instead of correcting his behavior, he simply got *better* at committing

Chapter Seventeen - The Apple and the Tree

crimes.

When Satan gets a foothold in a person, he doesn't stop there. He worms his way in until he seeps out of that person and into those around them. He starts with those closest to them, their friends and family, but he's never satisfied. He keeps moving, keeps working, until he gets a stranglehold on a whole area.

We saw his influence in our tiny community. Police made drugs busts left and right, sending many to jail. The bigger drug dealers had the money to get themselves out, but the regular users typically didn't. This led to a string of break-ins – while they were locked up, someone would ransack their homes.

The drug lifestyle was, to say the least, not good on family relationships. I saw it weekend after weekend growing up. I saw the fights it caused between couples; I saw my dad soothe scared, displaced children when their parents were arrested. I never understood it – the drugs destroyed their family, yet I knew the statistics were against those children: they were likely to turn to a life of drugs themselves. But none of it hit me the way it did when I had to watch my own nieces follow in their father's footsteps.

Before I even realized what was really happening, Christina and Andrea were deep in the drug scene. Jeff and his two oldest daughters became closer than they had been in years, but unfortunately, it was meth that bonded them.

I've beat myself up over and over, wondering what I could have done or said to prevent it. Why didn't I see it coming? Why didn't I notice as soon as it started and...intervene somehow? But it wasn't that easy. For one thing, Christina hid it very well. When you see those before and after pictures of meth addicts, you see stringy, thinning hair and rotten teeth falling out. But Christina's physical appearance changed very little. She lost a little weight, but she wasn't very big before drugs, either, so it wasn't so noticeable. Her skin tone was still good. She took care of herself.

Andrea, on the other hand, changed almost immediately. Before drugs, she was a beautiful blonde with her dad's vibrant eyes – the eyes he had before drugs stole their shine. But within a couple months of using meth, her looks changed. Not like those photos with festering facial sores and missing teeth; the change in Andrea was much less dramatic. It was hard to explain the way her face morphed, somehow, but people noticed. In fact, when Jeff had been locked up and hadn't seen his daughter in a few months, he didn't recognize her when he saw her. He was in the home of a drug dealer when Christina walked inside. As he glanced out the window, he saw Andrea sitting in the passenger seat of Christina's car. He stopped and stared out at his own daughter and asked, "Who's out there in your car, Christina?"

As little girls, Christina and Andrea had such a loving relationship with Jeff. Some of my best memories include watching him chase them around the yard all those years ago while they squealed with delight when he caught them. He hoisted them off the ground and held them in the air over his head while they giggled, their little arms reaching for the safety of their daddy's neck. When he lowered them, they would wrap themselves around Jeff, their tiny foreheads resting against him while they begged, "Again! Again!"

He did everything with those girls when they were small. He dressed up and played princesses with them. He taught them how to fish and hunt. He cheered them on during their t-ball games and went to their school plays.

When drugs took over, he all but disappeared from their lives. If he was in prison, they felt their dad's absence. But even when he was out, he wasn't the same man they knew when they were little. And I *knew* that. I knew he didn't take care of them the way he should have, the way they needed him to. But they had a strong support system in the rest of our family. They were loved and taken care of. When Jeff wasn't providing for them, we picked up his slack however we could.

Looking back, I'm not sure why their addiction to meth came as such a shock to me. As I said before, the statistics were against them. But I guess I just thought the pain their dad caused them, caused all of us, would be enough to keep them far away from it. I guess I thought if they were unhappy or looking for some kind of escape, they would *talk* to one of us. But that was foolish of me. What young person is going to warn an adult that she's thinking about using drugs? There must have been other signs,

signs I missed while wrapped up in all the drama and devastation that had come to my life. Unfortunately, those girls had to deal with all the same drama and devastation I did. They just chose a different outlet to deal with it all. And because I missed those signs, whatever they might have been, I will forever feel that I failed my nieces. That's a hard thing to live with.

I watched, helpless, as Jeff and his daughters became inseparable once again. Their lifestyle became very unstable, with the girls moving in and out, staying with him and Shayla for a while and then all four of them would go stay at someone else's house for a week or longer. There were no roots. They followed the drugs, wherever they might take them.

Christina told me years later the four of them would use meth together, sometimes staying up for anywhere from three to ten days straight without even realizing it. It was a euphoric world where they lost track of the concept of time. She once looked at a Facebook picture she had posted and realized she was still wearing the same clothes she had on in that picture, though the date was two days before. Meth had a hold on all of them, and they lived in a whirlwind that spun around it.

But with a life like that, none of them could hold down an actual job. So Jeff, who had taught his daughters how to throw a baseball, how to bait a fishing hook, now taught them how to steal without getting caught. He broke Christina in at Walmart, where he helped her steal two knives. If he felt anything at all – fear, adrenaline, remorse – he was a master at hiding it. He remained cool and collected, strolling out of the store with those knives tucked in his and Christina's waistbands, almost daring the employees to stop them.

They spent their nights out prowling, stealing items they could trade for drugs, their goal simply to have enough money to continue to feed their addictions. The local Walmart took the biggest hit. They stole almost nightly, pooling their loot to trade for enough meth to get them by one more day.

Sometimes their exploits went beyond a few miscellaneous items at Walmart. When one local woman went to prison, Jeff, Shayla, Andrea, and her boyfriend broke into her house. They stole everything they possibly could, even the washer and dryer.

They spent hours in that house without fear, making multiple trips to unload their loot until the house was empty.

But no one can live a life like that for too long without things falling apart underneath their feet. Any "bond" Jeff and the girls may have formed started to crumble as all four of them began to turn on each other. They accused each other of stealing. Soon, the father-daughter relationship no longer existed; it was addict versus addict. The fights amongst them all became vicious. Dangerous.

And before Jeff even knew what hit him, he found himself separated from Shayla. She got an order of protection against him, and he literally lost almost everything he owned. His belongings could fit in a trunk of a car. He stored his stuff in a small corner at Stan's. He had no home, no job, and no wife. Christina had a small house, and he sometimes stayed with her, though the two of them roamed around town, following the drugs, staying with various people a few nights at a time. He didn't even ask me or anyone else for a place to stay – he knew he wasn't trusted.

I knew what was going on, but by this point, I had no idea how to even attempt to stop it. After years of attempting and failing to help my brother, I was at a loss. Trying to talk to Jeff or my nieces about it seemed pointless; they were in too deep to listen to any voice of reason. And so, I did the only thing I knew how to do, the only thing that gave me any power over the situation: I prayed for them.

Chapter Eighteen
A Desperate Plan

One cold, blustery Friday night in January 2015, Lori and I watched TV in the living room. We both yawned in our recliners. I looked up at the clock on the wall. Ten thirty. I opened my mouth to announce I was ready to retire for the night when a knock on the door interrupted me.

Lori and I both sat up, exchanging worried glances as the typical-parent thoughts ran through our minds. Who would be at our house, knocking on the door so late? Were the kids okay? The grandkids?

But when I looked through the peephole and saw my brother standing there, my stomach rolled. Had something happened? Were the girls okay?

I yanked the door open. "Jeff. What's going on?"

He gave me a weak smile. "Hey, big brother. Sorry it's late. You guys weren't in bed, were you?"

"No. Is everything okay?"

He strained to look behind me. "Yeah, yeah, everything's fine. Just...wanted to come by. Talk. You know, catch up a little. That okay?"

My stomach flipped again. *Okay, no one's hurt. But...is there any cash laying around? Any prescriptions that need to be hidden?* Funny how when the biggest fear was alleviated, so many little ones jumped to the surface.

I moved out of the doorway. "Yeah, of course. Come in."

Lori appeared in the kitchen and took a seat at the table. "Sit down, Jeff." I couldn't help but smile as Jeff sat down across from my wife. I loved her even more at that moment, if it was possible. It didn't matter how many times he had hurt me, had hurt our family, she still welcomed him into our home.

I sat down at the end of the table. "So, what's up?"

He sighed. "I saw Shayla with another man."

Lori and I exchanged glances.

"Last night. At the bar. She didn't know I was there. She...she left with him."

I sucked in a breath. "Um, I...I'm sorry."

He swallowed, and I could see he was fighting back tears. "I know you probably don't believe me, but...I really loved her. I thought...I don't know. I thought we'd get through this." He looked down at the table. "I just...things have been...crazy. You know?"

This time, I held Lori's gaze for a moment. My mind raced. Jeff had clearly come to do more than just 'catch up a little.' There was so much I wanted to say, but I knew I had to be careful with how I said it. I didn't want to lecture him, didn't want to beat him down when he was clearly already low. "Um, yeah, Jeff. They have been."

"Christina and Andrea, they're...they're a mess, you guys. They're ten times worse than I ever thought about being."

I sat up straighter, surprised by his words. I studied him. He wasn't fidgeting. His eyes weren't darting around the room, but stayed focused on his hands that rested on the table. He appeared to be sober – a look I hadn't seen on him in a long time. And in that rare moment of sobriety, he was able to look back over his shoulder and see his daughters going as fast as he was. And what could he do? How could he help them when he couldn't even help himself?

"I'm sorry to hear that, Jeff." I already knew the girls were in over their heads, but hearing it come from Jeff only made it more real. My throat tightened. "I hate to see the girls like this."

"We pray for them every day," Lori added gently.

Jeff took a deep breath and exhaled slowly. "I can't find a job. No one around here will give me a chance."

I bit my lip. *How many chances have you been given? Chances you blew over and over again?* He didn't seem to remember those.

As he sat at that table, trying to hatch a plan for his future that didn't include Shayla, Lori and I just listened. It was clear he had a lot weighing on his mind, and he needed to talk, needed to get it out.

Chapter Eighteen - A Desperate Plan

When he stopped talking, I racked my brain for some advice. He was depressed and tired of fighting, and I knew in his state of mind, if I said the wrong thing, he would close up and shut me out all over again. I spoke slowly, choosing my words carefully. "Jeff, you've got to keep your head up. Keep marching. The girls…they need you to get clean. If you keep trying, things will work out."

He nodded, but seemed to have barely heard me. As I sat there, staring at this defeated fifty-one-year-old man, my chest ached. This wasn't my goofy, fun-loving brother. Everything was different. It wasn't like old times. There was no laughter, no stories of our childhood. We didn't talk about hunting or fishing, about Dad or Mom or our memories with them. His life was falling apart, and I had no idea how to help him put it back together. I barely knew him anymore, and I didn't know how to help him.

By twelve thirty, the conversation began to fizzle. Heavy pauses filled the air, with all three of us at a loss for words. I stifled my yawns.

Lori pushed her chair away from the table quietly. "I think I'll head to bed, if that's okay with you two."

"It's okay. I'm keeping you guys up." Jeff ran his hands through his hair. "I should be going soon."

"No, don't…you don't have to rush off. I'll stay up." I wasn't ready to let him go just yet. When would I see him again? When would I have the chance to sit down with him like this, just the two of us?

As I searched once again for some words of encouragement, something to inspire my brother to pull himself together and start over, Jeff leaned forward on his elbows. "I will never go back to prison."

My eyebrows shot up. "What?"

He shook his head. "I will never go back to prison. I…I can't. Not again."

The sleep-craving fog in my head lifted as I processed his words. What did that mean? That he was going to clean himself up? Get some help? Would he finally steer his boat off the collision course and quit running into things?

"I swear, if I ever get arrested again, I'll…I'll hang myself. Or

I'll do something to...to make the cop shoot me."

My hope, however short-lived, was crushed. He had no intentions of staying away from trouble. A knot pulled in my chest as I realized what he'd really just said: he'd rather die than go back to prison.

The thought of my brother taking his own life was devastating. But what bothered me even more at that moment was the other threat he'd made – the one about making a cop shoot him. After spending so much of my life around law enforcement, I knew that a cop would only shoot if they felt threatened. "Jeff, I..." My eyes narrowed. "What do you mean, 'do something to make the cop shoot'? What...what would you do?"

He shrugged. "I don't know. Maybe I'll get ahold of a gun a shoot first."

I stared at him. "Why? Why would you do that to someone? Why would you put that on a person's conscience?"

He leaned back against his chair. "Because...I'm not going back to prison."

My stomach churned. I'd known for a long time that he no longer loved or respected himself. But at that moment, as I sat speechless across from him, I realized he no longer loved or respected *anyone*. Not Dad, not Jackson. The drugs had taken away his humanity, leaving this shell of a man who didn't care about anyone or anything.

I lay in bed that night after he left, my eyes wide open. Would he really pull a gun on a police officer? What if my dad had been put in that situation? And Jackson, who was just starting his career...what if he found himself facing someone like Jeff? Someone so reckless, so determined to avoid jail time that he forces someone to kill him? Even though the shooting would be justified, it would still weigh on his conscience forever.

I tossed and turned, pushing the covers away and then pulling them back on. The Saline County police were used to Jeff and his antics, and tended to be almost relaxed around him. *Oh, Jeff got caught buying drugs again. Or, Jeff's been stealing again.* They knew him. They had already arrested him more than once. What if they let their guard down the next time they encountered him and someone was hurt or even killed?

Chapter Eighteen - A Desperate Plan

My cousin was the chief of police. Wasn't it my duty, my responsibility, to warn him of my brother's intentions? To make the local police aware? To let them know their lives may be in danger?

Something pulled inside my chest. Strange, thinking of Jeff more as a criminal than as my own brother. When did that happen? All those years I spent worrying about Jeff, trying to protect him, and now I was trying to protect others *from* him.

I got up out of bed so my restlessness wouldn't wake Lori. In the living room, I paced. He had given up. And something bad was coming; I could feel it inside of me. I didn't want to lose my brother. Despite everything that had happened, I loved him more than I could put into words. The idea of him harming himself, as he'd threatened to do, made my stomach lurch until I doubled over, pulling my knees to my chest in the middle of the floor.

But again, I pictured Jackson. My son, out there on the streets, trying to protect people in our broken society. The thought of someone out there, someone like Jeff, pulling a gun on him made my blood turn cold. Each police officer out there, just trying to do his job, is someone's son. Or daughter. Or husband. Or wife. Or daddy. Or mommy.

I peeled myself off the floor and almost crawled back to my bed. My body felt weak, but inside, I was resolved. I knew what I had to do.

The next morning, I called my cousin, the Harrisburg Chief of Police. With tears streaming down my face, I recounted the conversation I'd had with my brother the night before.

He listened. When I finished, silence filled the line for several moments before he finally sighed. "Thank you, Jack. Thanks for letting us know."

I swallowed. When I spoke again, my voice cracked. "I just...this wasn't an easy phone call to make, you know? But I thought...I mean, I wanted to warn you, in case..."

"I know." He sighed again. "You did the right thing. I hate it that you had to...I'm sorry it's gotten to this point."

I closed my eyes. "Me too."

When I hung up the phone, I dropped to my knees in the middle of the kitchen floor. "God, please…" But I didn't even have the words to pray. Faces flashed through my mind. Jeff. Jackson. My dad. Christina. Andrea. A young boy with streaks of dirt on his cheeks, peeking out through a clouded window as his dad was put inside the back of my dad's squad car – arrested for drugs. What had become of that little boy after all these years? Had he escaped that life? Had he found a way out of that world of destruction and devastation?

I leaned forward and pushed my head in my hands, trying to erase the image from my mind. "God, I just…I need you. Jeff needs you. The girls, they need you. Please…" And from somewhere within me, a new prayer emerged, one I hadn't said before. "Give me strength. For whatever is coming. I can't do this by myself – I can't handle it anymore. I give it to you. I give all of this to you. I just ask you give me Your strength to get through it."

Chapter Nineteen
A Battle Lost

I didn't know it at the time, but while I tossed and turned in bed that night after Jeff's visit, while I cried and paced the floors and searched my heart for what I should do next, my brother made a middle-of-the-night trip to Walmart. He had one mission: to steal something he could sell or exchange for drugs. The particular item he chose that night was a chainsaw.

To this day, I will never know how he managed to get a chainsaw out the doors of Walmart without getting caught. The fact he did it only reiterates my point that when it came to stealing, Jeff was a professional. Where could you possibly tuck a large item such as a chainsaw as you walked past employees and out the big, brightly-lit exit? Somehow, he pulled it off.

However, a loss prevention officer happened to notice the theft while reviewing video footage a couple days later. They called the police, and unbeknownst to Jeff or any of us, a warrant was issued for my brother's arrest. Lori and Tiffany even saw him standing outside with the chainsaw, the same day the warrant went out, as they drove by a house where he and Andrea often hung out. They had no idea he'd stolen it just days prior.

The following Saturday – a week since he'd stolen the chainsaw – Jeff went to the Saline County Detention Center to ask an officer to accompany him to Shayla's house so that he could pick up some of his things. With the order of protection she had against him, Jeff wasn't allowed to be around her without an officer present. But minutes after he walked inside, he was charged with theft.

A huge weight lifted from my shoulders when I heard he'd been taken to jail that morning – peacefully, with no confrontation. I still held on to that same mentality: jail was a safe place for him. A place where he'd stay out of trouble. For the first time since he'd visited me that night, I slept soundly. That bad feeling in the pit of my stomach eased. He'd gone to jail, and no one had been hurt in the process. Maybe all that talk at my kitchen table was just that – talk.

Little did I know, my brother was still determined that he wouldn't spend any more of his time behind bars.

On Tuesday, February 10, 2015, I left an ordinary day at work. I got in my truck, cranked up the radio and sang along loudly to pass the time as I drove from Madisonville, Kentucky, back home. I almost didn't hear my cell phone when it rang. The caller ID told me it was Randy Nyberg, the Saline County Circuit Clerk.

Randy and Dad were good friends and I'd known Randy for years, but I always felt a little twist in my gut when I saw his name on my phone: he was the one who called me to tell me about my Dad. I swallowed the small lump that jumped in my throat as I turned the radio down and answered the phone. "Hello, Randy. How are you?"

Silence. It was just a moment, but I knew immediately that something was wrong by the small hesitation. "Hey, Jack."

I sat up straighter and shut the stereo completely off. "What's going on?"

He sighed. "Are you...I'm afraid I need to tell you something. Can you get to a good place so we can talk privately?"

My heart raced. "I'm alone in my truck, Randy. Go ahead."

Pause. "You better pull over, Jack."

I pulled over on the side of the road, my pulse pounding in my ears. I put the truck in park and cleared my throat. "Okay. Go."

"Jack, it's Jeff. He...he hung himself in his jail cell. They transported him to the hospital, but...things don't look good."

A wave of nausea rolled through me. *Oh no, oh no, oh no. He didn't. He couldn't.* I pictured him sitting at my kitchen table that night, pictured the defeated look in his eyes. I knew he was giving up, but I still thought...I still hoped...

"Jack, are you still there? Can you hear me?"

I sat up straighter. "Um, yeah, Randy. I hear you. So he's..." I swallowed. *Pull it together.* "He's still alive?"

"He's in the hospital. They tried to revive him at the jail and called an ambulance. But…you better get down there as soon as you can. I'm so sorry, Jack."

My ears rang. I leaned my head against the steering wheel. "Thanks for calling me, Randy. I've gotta get ahold of Lori."

I lowered my cell phone to my lap and squeezed my eyes shut, trying to force the dizziness to pass so I could get back on the road. I was still about thirty minutes from home. Randy's words replayed in my mind. *You better get down there as soon as you can.* I didn't know how much time I had, if any.

Please don't take him from me. Lord, I…please don't let this be the end. But even as the prayer went up, I knew, somehow, that it was. I just knew.

When I spotted an opening to get back onto the busy road, I took it. I called Lori and asked her to get ahold of Jeff's daughters. Then I called Stan. It was strange, relaying my phone call with Randy to both of them. I could hear myself telling them what Jeff had done, but my voice sounded foreign, like someone else was talking. I drove home, but it was as if my car was on autopilot. I don't remember any other vehicles on the road, don't remember making the turns taking me back to my hometown. I don't even remember pulling into the parking lot of the hospital or putting my truck in park before I leapt out and sprinted to the front door.

Inside, I took a deep breath. What would he look like? Would he be able to respond? Would he know I was there? What would I say to him? Would he even hear me? I knew I couldn't afford to waste any time, but my walk slowed to a crawl as I made my way toward the waiting room. I pleaded with God in my mind. *Lord, please. I know I don't deserve it, but I'm asking for a miracle.* I spotted Lori and Stan across the room, then Carol. My Aunt Linda, my dad's sister, who worked for the Sheriff's Department, along with her husband George, a former sheriff. *Please, just…just give me the words to say. Help me to let my brother know I love him, that I've always loved him. Help me to let him know I don't blame him. For any of it.*

But I never got the chance to say any of that. The Illinois State Police had taken over the investigation, including his body. When the detective told me I wasn't allowed to go in and see my brother, I crumpled like a rag doll. I wept on the cold, hard floor of the waiting room with Lori on one side of me and Stan on the other.

My brother passed away in the hospital that afternoon. All those demons he had carried around on his back for so long finally rode him to the ground.

It didn't seem real. As family members gathered around me, hugging me, offering consoling murmurs, I sat in numb shock. *This wasn't supposed to happen. Not to Jeff. Not to any of us.*

Though it upset me initially, I realized right away it was better I didn't see my brother that day. I wasn't upset with the detectives who wouldn't allow me inside the room; if anything, from the experience I had through all those years with my dad, I expected it. I knew the procedure. My last memory of him is the late-night visit, and I know now that the conversation we had, however upsetting it may have been, was his way of telling me he was tired of fighting those demons.

His funeral was packed. A huge crowd of people came out to pay their respects. There were people who had known him his whole life, had known our family. There were so many people who had tried to help him get back on his feet throughout the years by hiring him to do odd jobs.

Looking out into the audience was the one and only time I've ever been grateful I didn't have my mom and dad. I scanned the crowd, stopping right there to thank God neither of our parents were there to see it. Mom was still alive, but her dementia had only gotten worse over the years and mentally, she was no longer with us. She didn't know Jeff anymore and didn't understand what had happened. The way I lost my mom was totally different from the way I lost Dad, and in some ways, it was worse – there's nothing more frustrating, more devastating, than knowing your parent is right beside you, but she doesn't even recognize you. But for that moment, and only that moment, I was thankful.

As for Dad, I can't even describe the pain that took over inside me when he died. But as difficult as it is to endure the death of a parent, I can't even begin to imagine what the loss of a child must feel like. Jeff's suicide would have absolutely crushed our dad. No matter what happened, no matter how many times he tried and failed to help Jeff get on the right track, he never gave up on his son. What Dad gave him was the very definition of tough love – he refused to bail my brother out of jail or give him money that would enable him to use drugs – but he did everything he could to get Jeff back on his feet. He helped him find multiple job opportunities. He gave him food and helped him provide for his kids when he struggled. He did whatever he could to give Jeff a fighting chance, no matter how many times he'd been let down by his own son before. "Maybe this will be it," I once heard him say. "Maybe this thing, this very next thing I do, will get him to the turning point." That hope burned inside of him right up until the day he died. After I lost my dad, I told God how unfair it was that he took him before he ever got to see Jeff finally win his battle. But at that moment, I thanked Him because Dad didn't have to see his son lose the battle for the last time.

When I spoke at the funeral service, I chose to keep my speech lighthearted. I chose to focus on the part of my brother that God made – the good person, the good dad, the good brother. The one who loved with everything he had. I remembered that person well, though the drugs kept him buried, trapped somewhere deep inside. I did my best to paint a joyful picture of my brother.

But when I saw him in that casket, I fell apart. I couldn't help but see that other side of him, the side that had ultimately taken over and defeated him. That's when the reality truly set in. *I lost my little brother.* But the truth was, I'd lost him long before then. I stared at him, this man who had become a stranger to me toward the end. That's what addiction does: it steals the soul inside that God created. As I saw him lying there, I couldn't help but think to myself, *This is where it ends for so many.* When addiction takes over, there are two ends, two walls – prison or death. My brother hit them both.

I don't blame God for my brother's fate; addiction is not of him but of our enemy. I know God made Jeff with a purpose in mind, one he never truly got to realize. The drugs clouded his mind and his decisions, sending him down a path never intended for him.

My Brother's Keeper

The Bible tells us in the book of John our enemy comes "to steal, and to kill, and to destroy." And in the case of my brother, that's exactly what he did. He got a foothold on Jeff and used it to grind him into the dirt.

But Satan wasn't finished – he never is. He's a ruthless enemy. Taking Jeff from us was only the beginning. Addiction runs rampant, destroying those under its control along with everything and everyone in their path. And that's the devil's plan: to take the life not just of one person, but of everyone he can along with that person.

Jeff's death felt like the end for me. After all those years of worrying and praying, a heavy silence settled in my mind. Jeff wasn't the only one who had lost the battle; I had, too. We all had. We couldn't protect him, couldn't keep him from the destruction he chose.

But what I didn't realize as I grieved for my brother was that the battle wasn't over. The months following Jeff's death brought more struggles, more heartache to not only our family but our entire community.

144

Chapter Twenty
Sins of the Father

Satan used Jeff's suicide to spur a chain of events.

Four more people in our community committed suicide throughout the sixteen months following Jeff's funeral. Every single one of those suicides were drug- or alcohol-related.

All of Jeff's family and close friends struggled to deal with the new reality we lived in, the one that didn't include him. No one took it harder than Stan, who had stayed by his side through all the ups and downs, through the betrayal and the heartache. We all beat ourselves up, wondering what we could have said or done that might have made a difference. But I think what bothered me – what still bothers me – most of all was the fact I was so naïve when it came to my nieces. Why didn't I take a more active role in their younger years? Why didn't I realize they were in danger and being neglected before I did? Why did I sit back and allow Andrea to stay with her dad when he was in no condition to take care of her? Lori and I tried to help – we took groceries to her every week and often gave her money. But why didn't we take her home with us? Why didn't I insist she move in with us, that all three of them move in with us, during those crucial years of adolescence? Maybe I couldn't have saved Jeff, but could I have made a difference for his daughters? For even just one of them?

I honestly believed that since the girls watched it all unfold, watched their dad fall apart time and time again, losing everything and almost everyone he loved, they wouldn't follow in his footsteps. But for whatever reason, all three of them gravitated toward the same path. All three girls, in their late teen and early adulthood years, chose the same life of addiction that took their father from them.

The girls took their father's death really hard, naturally. Regardless of what he had done, he was still their dad. Losing him impacted all three of them and the choices they made from there. For his youngest daughter, Megan, it was a turning point. Megan got into drugs and found herself in trouble for stealing in a neighboring county. Since she was a first-time offender, she got off on probation and was able to get into to a nine-month rehabilitation center – Ladies Living Free, a Christian-based facility in Paducah, Kentucky. I believe this was the best possible choice for her – in my experience, going to a local, thirty-day rehab facility is a waste of time. I wouldn't say they are never beneficial, but for someone addicted to meth, thirty days simply isn't enough time. And if going away to rehab is a possibility, I believe it's the best thing to do. A complete change of environment. Miles away from what's familiar, including those friends and family the addict knows are nearby and may be tempted to check out to run back to. For Megan, going away for an extended time proved to be most effective.

Megan got a good job while in the program. She met a great guy, and they married shortly after she completed the nine months. She and her new husband lived and worked near Ladies Living Free, so Megan continued to be part of their program. They soon welcomed a baby girl and she quit her job to be a stay-at-home mom. Life couldn't have been better for Megan and her new little family.

I wish the story ended there, with that "happily ever after." Unfortunately, it doesn't. About six months after their daughter was born, odd things started happening and her explanations for them just didn't add up. Her husband later said he wasn't sure what was going on, he could just tell something wasn't right. I knew exactly what he meant by that; I'd experienced that same feeling over and over again for twenty years with Jeff. One Sunday afternoon, he couldn't find Megan and their daughter in the place where she'd promised they would be. She wouldn't answer her phone. Frantic, he began calling everyone they knew, hoping someone had seen her or knew where she might be. While in the process of searching for her, he got a call from the sheriff's department in a Kentucky county just across the state line, asking him to come and get his daughter. Megan had been arrested for DUI, endangerment of a child, and possession of meth.

Her husband was floored by her charges. He had absolutely no idea she was using again. But as he drove to pick her up, pieces of the puzzle that had been the last six months began to fall into place. When she needed extra money and her explanation didn't quite add up…when bills didn't get paid and she had excuses that didn't make sense…days he couldn't get ahold of her and she claimed she never received his missed calls, though her phone seemed to work just fine.

Megan was arrested again one week before she was due to get off on of probation for her earlier escapades that led to her initial arrest. Sitting in jail, she missed her daughter's first birthday party. She is likely going to receive prison time, especially since she was still on probation at the time of her arrest. I am so thankful her husband is there to love and take care of their daughter, and I know he will work hard to provide a good life for her. I pray Megan has spent her time in jail thinking about where she's at, how she got there, and how good she had it before she went back to meth. I pray she will get her life back together before it's too late, before she misses anymore of her daughter's life.

Andrea, Jeff's middle daughter, found herself on the verge of her own "happily ever after." When she managed to clean up, she lived in a nearby town with her husband and three sons. They had a beautiful, happy home. But when she watched her older sister continue to struggle with meth and reached out to her, spending time with her in attempt to help her, she ended up back into drugs as well. She left her husband and all three boys. For the past three years, she's bounced from boyfriend to boyfriend and house to house, never living in the same place for more than a few months. She's been arrested for theft twice, but somehow managed to work her way out of trouble both times. One of her ex-boyfriends who happened to be with her at the time of one arrest ended up going to prison for it, while her charges were dropped. She's spent a few weeks in jail, waiting for someone to raise enough bail money to get her out, but she's avoided any lengthy confinement.

To this day, Andrea refuses to admit that she has a drug problem. She's very convincing when she says she's clean. But to hang out in the places she chooses, surrounding herself with the people she does, it simply isn't possible. She doesn't have much to do with her three boys, but fortunately, they have good homes. The two youngest boys, Joseph and Michael, live with their respective fathers. The oldest, Byron, lives with his ex-stepdad, who is Michael's biological dad. Byron wanted to stay in his hometown and go to school there with his friends and his ex-stepdad fought to make it happen for him, which says a lot about the person he is. Byron comes and stays with us on weekends frequently and often goes with us on short trips. Byron and Michael live in a warm, stable environment. Joseph, the middle son, also has a good home, surrounded by a steady, loving family. I am so thankful that God has provided them with people who love them and want the best for them. My only regret is that Andrea is missing all of it. The boys are missing out on a lot of memories they should be making with their mom, and since they can't all three live together, they're missing out on memories together as well.

Christina, the oldest, moved in with us after Jeff died and we did everything we could to help her get straightened out. She had been in trouble as well – same old story, drug and theft charges – and had done two court-ordered thirty-day stints in rehab that were essentially a waste of time. She came out of both of them and went straight back to meth. By the time she moved in with us, she had lost everything, including her four beautiful children and her nursing degree.

After Megan completed the nine-month program at Ladies Living Free and seemed to be doing so well, we convinced Christina she needed to go. She was on probation and had tested positive for meth, so her probation officer had basically told her if she didn't go into the program at LLF, she would likely go to prison. Megan was still involved in the program at the time and helped us get Christina in. The day before she was to enter the program, we sat her down for a difficult conversation.

"Christina," I began, then sighed, trying to choose my words carefully. "We want so much more for you. More than this life you've been choosing for yourself. This program…it can help you find the life you're meant to have."

She nodded, barely meeting my eyes. I knew she didn't want to go, but she realized she didn't have much choice. The alternative – time in prison – wasn't what she wanted, either.

"It's not going to be easy," I acknowledged. "For the first two weeks, you won't be able to make any phone calls at all. After those two weeks, you can call us any time you have the chance. And we'll be thrilled to hear from you." I swallowed, hardening my face. "But if you call us and ask us to come pick you up before you complete the program...we will not come and get you. If you don't finish those nine months, you're on your own."

Her head jerked up, her eyes wide.

"I'm serious, Christina. This program...it's a great opportunity. They can help you get back on your feet. They can help you find a job so you can support yourself. They can give you the resources you need to help you stay clean and beat this once and for all. But if you're not willing to stick it out, to put in the work when things get tough, then...we can't keep doing this. We can't let you stay here, stuck in the same old rut, never moving forward. I just..." I closed my eyes, fighting the tears that threatened. "I can't watch you go any further down that path. Because I know how it ends. And so do you."

I opened my eyes to meet hers. And for the first time in a long time, I saw something soften in her. She nodded, knowing exactly what I meant.

Lori drove her down there the next day. When they pulled into the parking lot, Lori hugged her tightly and prayed for her. But before she got out of the car, Lori squeezed her hand. "Remember, Christina, you have to stick this out. If you don't, for any reason, we will not come and pick you up."

"I know." Christina looked down at her lap. "I know."

We didn't expect to hear from her for a while, knowing she wouldn't be allowed to make any calls those first two weeks. So when Lori's phone rang after thirteen days and we saw LLF's number on the caller ID, her heart sank. "Hello?"

"Lori?" Christina's broken voice was barely audible.

Lori leapt to her feet. "Christina? Are you okay?"

She sighed. "I'm...I'm okay. I just...I've been kicked out. Of the program. Can you…will you please come and get me?"

Tears sprang to Lori's eyes and fell silently down her cheeks. She lowered herself back into her chair, her stomach in knots. And then, she said the most difficult word she's ever had to say: *"No."*

Tough love is one of the hardest things to give. But we knew we had to stand our ground. We couldn't let her come back to our home, only to let her fall back into the same pattern she'd been living in for so long. We wouldn't be helping her by enabling her to stay on drugs. We had to let her fail, as difficult as it might be to do so.

The lady in charge of the Ladies Living Free program was too kind to just kick her out on the street, so she got her some food and paid for one night in a hotel room in Paducah. Megan went and picked her up the next day and took her to a homeless shelter in Marion. Christina had been ordered to call her probation officer within twenty-four hours if she did not complete the LLF program for any reason, so she did. They set up an appointment to meet so Christina could figure out what she would do next.

However, she talked to her mother, Kimberly, who still lived in Florida, and Kimberly wired her money for a bus ticket so she could come down there. She failed to show up for her appointment with her probation officer. In Florida, she started dating a man and was soon back on meth. She eventually got arrested for violating an order of protection he got against her.

As she sat in jail in Florida, Saline County also issued a warrant for her arrest because she didn't show up to her appointment with her probation officer as ordered. So, after she served her time, Saline County sent someone down there to pick her up and bring her back to Southern Illinois. They revoked her probation, which was for possession of meth, and sent her to prison for three years. She gets credit for time served in jail before sentencing, plus she qualifies for the drug rehab program while incarcerated, which knocks time off if completed. Plus, in the prison system, she will get a day knocked off for every day of good behavior, so she's due to be paroled in August 2018.

Again, I regret that she's missing so much of her children's lives, but I am thankful they have good homes filled with people who love them and take care of them. Her two youngest daughters live with their father. Her son is also able to live with his dad. Her oldest daughter lives with her grandmother – Jeff's ex-wife, Abigail, who raised Christina all those years as her own. She is a senior in high school, preparing for college. All four of her kids are doing well, being raised by people who are doing everything they can to keep them on the right track. They harbor some ill feelings toward their mother, and who can blame them? Growing up without their mother present in their lives is never easy on children. So many things they've missed out on – and continue to miss out on – because of her choices.

It's difficult to comprehend what would have made Jeff's daughters go down that road. One would think in the war against drugs, there would be no bigger advocates than his three girls. Growing up, they watched meth tear their homes apart over and over again. They watched their father lose everything he had. I know their childhood wasn't easy and my brother is largely to blame for that. It makes my stomach roll to think of the chaos they must have seen growing up, to think of the many times they must have felt so confused. So neglected. So unloved. But they also understood the source of their pain. They remembered their real father, the man he used to be before drugs took over his life. Why would they choose to let it take over their own lives in the same way?

They had so many opportunities to choose a different life. They received so many blessings. If those things weren't enough to keep them from meth, will anything ever be? Will anything ever help them truly beat it? That's what's so dangerous about meth: once it gets ahold of a person, it's nearly impossible to shake it. Addicts watch everything fall apart all around them, but just don't care enough to fix it. The meth wraps itself around their brain until it overtakes it. It skews their thought process, causing them to lose sight of what actually matters, like their families. Their children.

One rehab counselor suggested that brain development in meth addicts actually stops or even goes backward, reverting to an almost childlike state, in some ways. We saw this with Christina in her inability to see the consequences of her actions. She moved in with us after Jeff died, and following a dirty drug test, her probation officer explained her choice was between jail and rehab. She chose rehab, knowing if she didn't make it through the program, she'd go to jail. But just days into the program, a counselor called Lori. "We can't get Christina to get out of bed and come to class. She's very uncooperative, and if her behavior doesn't change, she will unfortunately be kicked out of the program."

When we got Christina on the phone, I tried to talk some sense into her. "Christina, I don't know how else to put this: if you don't get up and go to class, you'll be back in jail. Is that what you want?"

She considered this. "No," she said finally, her voice small.

"Then get up. Get ready. Do what the counselors tell you to do."

She sighed. "Okay."

When we hung up the phone, I shook my head, bewildered. Why did we have to talk her through it? She chose rehab over jail, determined not to go back. So why didn't she realize failure in rehab would mean time in jail? Why couldn't she see for herself her actions have consequences?

But meth seems to block any complex thought process. It keeps people from thinking about anything other than themselves and what they need right then, at that moment, to feel good. They can't seem to see consequences, can't seem to see how their actions will impact them or anyone else. That's why they can steal and hurt the people they love. Meth just shuts off that part of the brain, the part that is able to rationalize, "What happens if I get caught?"

I believe with all my heart no one can beat it on his own, but there is hope: God, and only God, makes it possible. Ladies Living Free is such a successful program, built on a Christian foundation. But when a person leaves there, she's fooling herself if she thinks she can continue her recovery without God. The temptation is just too big. Thankfully, we serve a God who is bigger! Through Him, and *only* through Him, all things are possible.

Chapter Twenty-One
Still Marching

That hole in my chest still gapes open; I feel my brother's absence in my life every day. Things I once loved to do, like hunting and fishing, will never bring the same joy.

I will never understand why it all happened. I can't count how many times I've wondered, *Why did this have to happen to Jeff? To our family? Why is this all on me?*

So many times, when I've wanted to give up, when I've wanted to crawl into bed and shut out the rest of the world for a while, I've heard my dad's voice in my head. "Always remember this, Jack: Life's tough, and it's not always fair. But the sun will still come up tomorrow. You have to get up and keep marching, even when you don't feel like it. Because someone is always counting on you." Those words he said to me all those years ago at my grandmother's funeral have never meant more to me than they do today. I have so many people counting on me every day – my wife, my kids, my grandkids, my boss, and above all else, God. I have to stay in the race.

To be honest, I still don't have the answers I seek. But I do know this: God never promised this life would be easy. In fact, the Bible tells us the opposite. In this broken world, we will all face trouble and loss, and God knows I've faced my share of it. I lost my dad to cancer. I lost my brother to addiction. In October 2017, I lost my mom – though the unfair, devastating truth is, I lost her to Alzheimer's long before that. In the midst of the trials I've faced, I've found victory, too: I've battled cancer, and with the help of my family and close friends, I survived. I've made so many mistakes along the way, and I'm so thankful for a God who doesn't give up on me, a God who loves me and gives me peace in the most unimaginable circumstances. A God who shows me beauty despite the darkness that surrounds me.

A God who allows me to seek Him and gives me His mercy, His love, His forgiveness, when I've done absolutely nothing to deserve it.

We all have a different journey to take in this world, and we will all face trials along the way. It's what we do in those trials that shapes us into the person we become. It's so tempting to bottle up our struggles, to try to hide them away so others can't see our pain, our flaws. But I believe we need to share our stories – successes and failures alike – when faced with life's challenges. It is my hope that my story may help someone who is suffering, someone who is fighting the war on addiction through someone they love.

Addiction is a disease. And it doesn't have a particular class or type of people it affects; it is an equalizer. It can wrap its claws around anyone – rich or poor, black or white, educated or not. It doesn't care who you are or where you came from, doesn't care what kind of family you have or what kind of person you are. It worms its way in a person, never giving up until it consumes him and, if it can, his entire family right along with him.

I don't have some magic formula to offer someone who is trying to help an addict. What I *can* offer is advice, based on things I learned along the way. As I said before, I made so many mistakes. I can't even count the hours I've wasted wishing for the chance to go back and do things over again, wondering if something I might have said or done differently may have made the difference for Jeff or his daughters. Thankfully, God has forgiven me for those mistakes. And through Him, I'm learning to forgive myself as well. I only hope that by sharing my story, someone out there, even just one person, might take something from it.

One thing I learned is when someone you love struggles with addiction, you have to get into a sort of protection mode. It's so easy to let someone else's self-destruction take you down that dark path, too, but you can't allow it to. I missed out on things while my kids were growing up – not necessarily physically, but mentally – because my mind was so consumed by my brother and his struggles that I couldn't allow myself to enjoy the blessings God put right in front of me. I put myself and even my family at risk, trying to save Jeff from the choices he made and the world he immersed himself in. The reality was, it was never up to me to save him; that was between Jeff and God. As difficult as it might have been, the best thing, the most powerful thing, I could have given Jeff was prayer. I prayed for him with every ounce of my strength, but I struggled to truly let go and give it to God. I let it become my obsession until it destroyed my own peace.

It was easy for me as a kid, on the outside looking in, to see addiction for what it was. I watched it destroy marriages and forever alter the lives of the kids who were unfortunate enough to be caught in the middle of it. But being on the inside, watching my brother fall into its trap, was a whole different experience. It's so much harder to step back and see the truth for what it really is when the addict is someone you love so fiercely. I wanted more than anything to believe his problem with drug abuse wouldn't get the best of him. I wanted to believe that, because of who I knew he was deep down, he would continue to be the father his daughters needed. And because I wanted to believe in it so much, my mind let me go ahead and believe that.

And unfortunately, Jeff's daughters suffered for it.

I can't help but kick myself for being so naïve when his girls were young. I *knew* that when kids lived with an addict, they were in danger. Innocence is stolen from them as they endure neglect and often abuse. Why could I see that from afar, but miss it when it was right in front of my face? Why couldn't I have seen Jeff's situation for what it really was and step in to those girls' lives in a more active way? I was so convinced having his daughters around him would help him get back on the right track that it just didn't register what his addiction might have been doing to them. Out of all the things I struggle to forgive myself for, out of all the things I question and wonder *what if,* the role I played in the girls' lives plagues me most. I should have been in constant communication with all three of them, talking to them about their dad and what they were feeling. I should have put them in contact with counselors, people who could offer them help getting through it all. I should have insisted Andrea move out as soon as I realized she was being neglected. Instead of taking her groceries and slipping her cash, I should have packed her things and taken her home with me.

One thing I learned from my dad, one thing I believe we actually did right despite all the things we might have done wrong, was to offer tough love when Jeff got himself in trouble. It was more difficult than I can describe to keep my face stone and try to ignore all the begging, the phone calls, the promises he made. Again, from the outside looking in, it seems like an easy thing to do. *Don't listen to the addict's pleas and promises. Stay tough.* But this wasn't just "some addict." It was my *brother*, my best friend. I wanted to help him however I could. I wanted to believe him when he promised to get clean. I wanted to believe he would change. But the reality is, if he wasn't willing to change his friends, his contacts, his scenery, nothing was going to change.

Growing up in the midst of the justice system taught me our actions have consequences. When an addict gets into trouble, he needs to pay his price like anyone else. If he finds himself in jail, let him stay there. It might sound strange, but despite what Jeff did, I still believe jail is the safest place for an addict. I don't blame the Saline County Detention Center for the choice Jeff made there. He was tired of fighting and determined to take his own life. It took months, maybe years, for me to admit this, but Jeff would have done what he did eventually no matter where he may have ended up.

Finally, and I believe this is the most important piece of advice I can offer, share Jesus whenever you can. If someone you love is struggling with addiction, especially with a powerful force like meth, Jesus is the only hope. Let's face it – Jesus is the only hope for any of us, no matter what our problems or issues might be. Relying on Him is the best way to get through this life. For a meth addict, it's the only way. Invite him to church. Tell him how Jesus can change his life and give him strength he never knew before. And pray for him as fervently as you can.

Jeff got a glimpse of life in Christ, but the devil was merciless. He never gave up, preying on my brother's weaknesses until he eventually overtook him again. It wasn't enough for Jeff – and it isn't enough for any of us – to just get a taste of Jesus. A one-time fix. It's a daily battle, a constant seeking of God. We can't get too comfortable. Our enemy is too smart, too cunning, and he'll swoop in as soon as we let down our guard.

Jeff, like so many others, lost his battle with the enemy. Being by his side, trying to fight that battle with him, to fight it *for* him, has shaped me into a different person today. But God is still good, and I will keep putting my hope in Him. With His help, I will continue to get up. I will stay in the race. I will keep fighting, focusing on all He has given me instead of what I've lost along the way.

And I will pray for those who, like me, find themselves fighting the ruthless enemy of addiction. As lonely as the battle may seem at times, we're never alone. We may lose the fight from time to time, but the Bible tells us who wins the war in the end. We will keep our heads up and keep marching, relying on the One who will bring us through it all.

Resources

Substance Abuse & Mental Health Services Administration (SAMHSA)
www.samhsa.gov
1-800-662-4357

Substance Abuse Treatment Locator (from SAMHSA)
http://findtreatment.samhsa.gov/

Partnership for Drug-Free Kids
https://drugfree.org
1-855-378-4373

National Institute on Drug Abuse
https://www.drugabuse.gov
301-443-1124

Cortland Prevention Services
http://www.cortlandprevention.org/
607-756-8970

The Meth Project
http://www.methproject.org/

Narcotics Anonymous
https://na.org/
818-773-9999

Adult & Teen Challenge
https://www.teenchallengeusa.com/
417-581-2181

Resources for Families Facing Alcohol and Other Drug Addiction (from Hazelden Betty Ford Foundation)
http://www.hazeldenbettyford.org/addiction/help-for-families/family-toolkit
1-800-293-8112

10 Tips to Help Family Members of Addicts Cope (from The Recovery Village)
https://www.therecoveryvillage.com/family-friend-portal/tips-help-cope/#gref
888-982-2747